DATE DUE

The Mystical Life of Jesus

SYLVIA BROWNE

The
MYSTICAL LIFE
of
✠ JESUS ✠

An Uncommon Perspective on the Life of Christ

DUTTON

DUTTON
Published by Penguin Group (USA) Inc.
375 Hudson Street, New York, New York 10014, U.S.A.
Penguin Group (Canada), 90 Eglinton Avenue East, Suite 700, Toronto, Ontario M4P 2Y3,
Canada (a division of Pearson Penguin Canada Inc.); Penguin Books Ltd, 80 Strand, London
WC2R 0RL, England; Penguin Ireland, 25 St Stephen's Green, Dublin 2, Ireland (a division of
Penguin Books Ltd); Penguin Group (Australia), 250 Camberwell Road, Camberwell, Victoria
3124, Australia (a division of Pearson Australia Group Pty Ltd); Penguin Books India Pvt Ltd,
11 Community Centre, Panchsheel Park, New Delhi – 110 017, India; Penguin Group (NZ),
cnr Airborne and Rosedale Roads, Albany, Auckland 1310, New Zealand (a division of Pearson
New Zealand Ltd); Penguin Books (South Africa) (Pty) Ltd, 24 Sturdee Avenue, Rosebank,
Johannesburg 2196, South Africa

Penguin Books Ltd, Registered Offices: 80 Strand, London WC2R 0RL, England

Published by Dutton, a member of Penguin Group (USA) Inc.

First printing, November 2006

1   3   5   7   9   10   8   6   4   2

 REGISTERED TRADEMARK—MARCA REGISTRADA

LIBRARY OF CONGRESS CATALOGING-IN-PUBLICATION DATA
Browne, Sylvia.
The mystical life of Jesus : an uncommon perspective on the life of Christ / Sylvia Browne.
p.   cm.
ISBN 0-525-95001-X (hardcover)
1.   Jesus Christ—Spiritualistic interpretations.   I. Title.
BT304.96.B76 2006
232.9—dc22   2006025306

Printed in the United States of America
Set in Bitstream Goudy Old Style
Designed by Amy Hill

While the author has made every effort to provide accurate telephone numbers and Internet
addresses at the time of publication, neither the publisher nor the author assumes any
responsibility for errors, or for changes that occur after publication. Further, the publisher does
not have any control over and does not assume any responsibility for author or third-party Web
sites or their content.

For my sons, Chris and Paul Dufresne,
and my dear friend, Linda Rossi.

Dearest Lord, look past the blindness of our eyes.

And help us see truth as the eons of time flies.

The values you taught reside in our soul.

Let the lessons of life, to love God be our goal.

Walk with us, Lord, through the harshness of life.

And smooth over all the innumerable strife.

I ask your blessing from God for everyone.

Especially since He in greatness sent His beloved son.

To my readers . . . bless you everyone.

Contents

Preface

I T IS VERY HARD sometimes to describe oneself, but as many of you know, I am what the world calls a psychic. I was born in Kansas City, Missouri, in 1936 and inherited my psychic gifts from my beloved grandmother and a long list of ancestors who had psychic abilities that go back more than three hundred years. In my youth I was tested many times by doctors and scientists, and they all came to the conclusion that I had very distinct paranormal abilities. They would throw terms at me such as clairvoyant, precognitive, clairaudient, prophet, sensitive and trance medium. While I more or less knew the definitions of these words, as a young woman I really didn't understand them that well, especially as they pertained to me. I just thought that maybe I was nuts or mentally ill.

As a young girl I would sense things, see things, and

hear things and sometimes they were very frightening to me. If it had not been for my grandmother Ada, I just think that I would have gone into a shell and locked myself out from the world. As it turned out, with my grandmother's loving counsel (and much, I'm sure, to the chagrin of my parents) . . . I didn't. I was nothing if not a handful—very precocious, outgoing, loud, energetic and incessantly asking questions and talking. My constant talking got me into trouble more times than not, as I would sense things and just blurt them out to family or even complete strangers. I really couldn't understand why my father would bury his face in his hands or why my mother would turn and yell at my father to do something with me. I'm sure it was hard on my family to raise me, for I would consistently do things that would embarrass them. Some may have seen my behavior as "cute" or "charming," but I am sure others would have just seen me as a little "brat."

I was eight years old when my spirit guide, Francine, first made contact with me. To hear the words "I come from God and you have nothing to fear" when no one was there was quite terrifying, and I immediately ran to my grandmother screaming. From that time on my gift of clairaudience has never left, and Francine would give counsel and solace to me many times over the years. She said to me in the beginning that she would not help me with my own abilities, as they needed to develop on their own, and to this day she does not help me with my private readings or in answering questions from audiences or groups when I do lectures.

I first became aware of my trance mediumship ability while taking a class on hypnosis in my late teens. Thankfully, I was with a few close friends whom I had grown up with and already had talked to them about Francine. The teacher started a group hypnosis exercise on the class, and I went under easily. Then, for the first time, Francine came into my body. She quickly introduced herself to my astonished friends and gave them a few tidbits of information so they would be convinced it was not me. When I came back to consciousness, my friends quickly informed me of what had happened and I instantly became infuriated. I was confused, angry and frightened. Francine immediately began talking to me to calm me down. She logically explained that she had to do this to show me my trance mediumship ability and that it was not harmful in any way. She knew I would never have allowed her to do it otherwise. The truth be told, she was probably right, as I was already in the mindset that I could possibly be crazy. We made a pact that day that she would never enter into my body in trance again without my permission . . . and she never has.

As most of you know, I have written many books on a variety of subjects dealing with spirituality and God and the paranormal. Much of the information in these books was heretofore unknown and comes from research trances with Francine. Over the years she has given me information that I have had transcribed into thousands of pages. Some of this information is very controversial and has caused me, as well as others, to research extensively for verification, as I have always been what I call an "open-minded skeptic." Most of the time I have been able to verify in varying degrees the information she has given me. Sometimes I cannot due to a lack of substantial documentation. I have found that many times it is a crapshoot at best because the farther you go back in time or history, the more obscure documentation becomes. You find yourself dealing with legends, myths, corruption, lies, deceit and traditions. So it is not always easy to verify her information. Much of what we think of as truth (historical or otherwise) has so many potential holes for untruth, you sometimes scratch your head in wonder as to why it is considered truth in the first place. This is especially relevant when you are researching and trying to get confirmation on religious subject matter.

Religion is so subjective and so steeped in traditional and historical beliefs that it is hard to discern and separate truth from fiction in many cases. Add to that the fact that all the major religions have bloody histories of corruption and schisms and holy wars, with different sects and factions constantly rising and falling, and you have the proverbial confusing and bewildering murky mess. Thank God that numerous scholars and writers and historians are taking a new interest in various religions, especially Christianity. With new discoveries being made in archaeology and with books like *The Da Vinci Code* by Dan Brown coming out, it has sparked a renaissance over the many controversies that have remained unanswered in Christianity and other religions.

With that in mind, when my publisher called me and

asked me to write a book on Jesus Christ and his life, I was stunned into disbelief and silence. I am nothing if not controversial already and my publisher wants me to write a book on our Lord? Being a Gnostic Christian, I am already considered heretical by most, but this assignment would really bring out the critics and skeptics and would be a daunting and often frightening task.

I then thought about my life for a bit. I had dedicated my life to God and to bringing forth the truth about our Creator by trying to help others through my books, my counseling and my lectures. I most surely have my faults, but I have tried to live a good life by helping others as much as I could. Would doing this book jeopardize all that I have tried to do for them? With what I know and believe, I would have to tell the truth as I know it, and that truth will create an inevitable controversy . . . but then, isn't that why I am here?

I have given my life to teaching and nurturing others, to helping people in any way I can for God. To write about such a holy figure as Jesus Christ may be madness on my part, but it would be an even greater madness to not put forth the truth about him and his works for God so that people can better understand his teachings and from whence he came. To that end, this book contains verifiable truths and where verification is not possible, it contains logical and truthful information from my spirit guide, Francine. In the more than sixty years of knowing and working with her, I have never found her to be untruthful in any way, and she brings with her the wisdom and knowledge of the Other Side.

In this book you will find many things that will "rattle your cage," "rock your boat" and "shake your tree" . . . in other words there are many things about Christ's life that I know to be true that fly in the face of the traditional teachings of Christianity. But truth is truth and you can feel it tangibly within your soul if you open yourself up to it. Close off from truth or don't acknowledge it and you will find yourself a slave to the powers of deception and lies and your soul will spiritually suffer. Christ said, "The truth will make you free" (John 8:31); but you have to *accept the truth* for it to make you free. I'm as free as a bird flying on the four winds . . . are you?

The Mystical Life of Jesus

CHAPTER 1

Birth and Childhood

THE LIFE OF Jesus Christ has been a topic of more books than anyone could count, let alone read. What I propose to do in this book is to give you real and researched facts according to the latest findings of scholars as well as information from the Other Side by my guide, Francine. In many cases they agree and in some cases they disagree; but the information will be put forth objectively so that the reader can come to his or her own conclusions. Much of the information from Francine is more than thirty years old and has been kept in safekeeping until the time was right for its release. Let me preface the following information right now so that there is no confusion—*by no means is any information given in this book meant to ever discredit the divinity of our Lord.* I have always and still do believe in the divinity of Jesus Christ, and none of the information put forth in this book in my opinion threatens that.

I just think it's timely to not only show the true story of Christ and his mission, but also how he lived and died as well as the true message he wanted to bring. In the telling of Christ's life, we will not just touch upon the three years of his life that most people know about, but we will also address the "lost years" of Jesus as well as other years that no one knows about.

The reader, as I always say, is welcome to take with him what he wants and leave the rest, but keep an open mind as to what I am about to relate about our Lord. I do feel in my heart that many of the facts and research will back up the knowledge that I will be giving, and then from your heart and soul you can make your own deductions.

Let's start at the beginning . . . Christ was not born in a manger. It's true that when he was born the Romans were taking a census and villages and cities were crowded with those who had to register according to the law. But even with the overcrowding, there were still rooms to be had at inns for the wealthy. Joseph was a direct descendent of the royal house of David (Matthew 1:1–16) and had to register both himself and his wife, Mary, at Bethlehem, which was called the city of David. Both Mary and Joseph were from royal and wealthy Judaic families and consequently Jesus was born in an inn and not in a stable with animals lying about. You must realize, contrary to what many teachings try to say, Jesus did not come from a poor, illiterate family.

The people of Bethlehem welcomed Mary and Joseph with great fanfare, and the fact that these two royal families had come together to produce an heir was quite a marvelous event. Israel at that time was a collection of small communities where word traveled fast through heralds and traveling minstrels. Most everyone quickly became aware of his birth and were thrilled. Many hoped that Christ was the Savior, for the prophecies of the ancient prophets said a king of royal lineage would grow up and free them from Roman bondage.

When Christ was born in the inn, the word spread that

these two people of royalty possibly gave birth to the Savior that prophecy foretold. Do you suppose, as portrayed in the Gospel of Luke, that a poor peasant family would have been admitted into the high temple to present Christ after he was born to be blessed and sanctified? No, because you had to give offerings and money to be admitted. So a royal family presented Christ at the temple. This was a country of small communities and like all communities people of like class stay together. These royal, wealthy families would socialize together, help each other, and have intermarriages between them, and that's how they all knew each other. Let's face it . . . we don't hobnob with Queen Elizabeth or even the Hiltons or Rockefellers. They keep to their own circles. The same as it is now, it was then.

Because Joseph was of royal lineage, he was not poor. He was an expert craftsman who attracted people from far and near to have him design and make their custom furniture. It would have been an honor for a customer to buy a magnificent design from a person with a royal bloodline. My spirit guide, Francine, says that Joseph had as many as thirty expert workers who helped build and sell his designs.

Before we go any further though, let's get into the conception of Jesus by Mary. The premise of a virgin birth by Mary is hotly contested by Biblical scholars. Liberal scholars take the view that the virgin birth of Jesus was pure mythology based on other pagan religions of the time. In Greek mythology, Zeus supposedly impregnated the virgin Danae by taking the form of a shower of gold, and the result was Perseus. He did the same with the virgin Semele, using a bolt of lightning, and the result was Dionysius. Horus, a major god of the Egyptian religion, was born of the virgin Isis and, coincidently, was also supposedly born in a stable. Mithra, the main god in Mithraism, which was a major religion of Rome, was conceived when God in the form of light entered a virgin. Myrrha was a virgin who gave birth to Adonis in Phoenician mythology. As you can see, the concept of a virgin birth was not new and its mythology permeated throughout cultures at the time.

Only the gospels of Matthew and Luke mention the virgin birth and both are dated by scholars after the Gospel of Mark and the Epistles of Paul. Neither Mark nor Paul mentions the virgin birth. Many scholars ask why not? Matthew bases his virgin birth story on the prophecy of Isaiah

(Isaiah 7:14); but that prophecy clearly states that the name of the child will be Immanuel, not Jesus. Many scholars believe that this prophecy actually refers to another child later on in Isaiah (Isaiah 8:3–4) and is not a prophecy concerning the Messiah. In fact, as we will see later on, many of the so-called prophecies concerning the Messiah are very dubious and have blatantly been misinterpreted. I am not saying this, but Biblical scholars are. Paul in Galatians (4:4) says, *"But when the time had fully come, God sent his son, **born of a woman,** born under the law, to redeem under the law, that we might receive the full rights of sons."* Most scholars say that the message here is that Jesus was a normal Jewish child called by God. If indeed Mary was a virgin, why not say so? Instead, he used the term woman.

As we will see throughout this book (as well as others on Jesus), many of the facts of Christ's life are based on the Bible. That is well and good to a point. After all, for many years it was the only source we had that had any substantial accounts of even a portion of Jesus' life. But most people have not done a lot of research on the Bible and how it came into being, just as they have not researched how Christianity came into being. The Bible is considered a holy book and the word of God by many Christians, but as many scholars have pointed out, the Bible can contain errors, inconsistencies and downright falsehoods!

We must remember that historically the Bible did not take its form until the Council of Nicaea in 325 A.D. That is some three hundred years after the life of Christ. Now, three hundred years is a long time, but on top of that we must also realize that it was put together by the early Catholic Church and was edited, rewritten, purged of what the early Church deemed heretical, and manipulated for their own agenda. Do you realize that even today no one knows *who actually wrote* the four gospels of the New Testament!

Biblical scholars believe that Matthew, Luke and Mark were written by the same writer, for the writing style is similar as are the stories, and that John was written by another writer because the writing style is different and also brings in new portions of Christ's life. I don't know about you, but I envision a little monk about a hundred or so years after Christ writing these stories that we know as the gospels of the New Testament. I am not going to go into a long treatise on how the Bible was written or put together other than to say that as far as the New Testament is concerned, its beginnings and writings are highly suspect, highly prejudicial, and were formulated and edited by the early Christian Church. In other words, as usual, man put his hand in it and messed it all up.

The Bible was written and edited in a time of extreme ignorance, in which the general populace was basically un-educated and illiterate. The early Christian Church was also at that time in the throes of formulation, with con-stant infighting and politics coming into play as Pauline Christians (those following the beliefs of Paul), Jewish Christians (those following the beliefs of Christ's brother James), and Gnostic Christians (those following the prem-ise of gnosis) vied for position and power within the Church structure. It all came to a head and was finally decided when the Roman emperor Constantine adopted Pauline Christianity as the Roman state religion in the early fourth century.

When Christians claim that the Bible is their source of truth for making extraordinary claims such as the virgin birth, then they must realize that the educated people of today (we are no longer dealing with an uneducated popu-lace) demand extraordinary proof. The old adage that "if it's in the Bible, it must be true" does not persuade all the followers anymore. Biblical scholars have found too many errors, lies and inconsistencies in the Bible for it to remain an unchallenged and *only* source for truth. Too many archaeological discoveries have been made that back up their findings and even put a whole new light on the time of Christ.

I do not depend upon the research of obviously biased Christian scholars, for their work is tainted with their beliefs; nor do I accept the biased work of skeptics or anti-Christian scholars. I always try to find more objective scholars who don't have an ax to grind one way or the other and who are really just looking for the truth. In this day and age, sometimes they are hard to find.

Getting back to the virgin birth of Christ, Francine says that it was not a virgin birth and that Joseph impregnated Mary. Francine further states that this does not take away Jesus' divinity because in reality God is the one who makes any impregnation possible for any child and chose Mary to be the mother of Christ—his direct report and messenger. That is probably a logical deduction in light of the fact that we all choose our own mothers and fathers when we incarnate, and I know of no virgin births that are on record as having taken place. Francine states that the writers of these gospels of Matthew and Luke used the mythology of virgin births to make the birth of Christ seem more divine and didn't want the mythology of other religions' virgin births superseding Christ's birth.

The Bible actually confirms this in a way. According to Matthew and Luke, Mary and Joseph were supposedly aware of the divinity of the child who would be born to her and also that they were to name him Jesus. Now, if this were so, why would they question Christ's actions? In Luke 2:42–51 we read about Christ in the temple at twelve years of age preaching to the teachers and how his parents, Mary and Joseph, had lost him and then found him preaching and rebuked him about his absence. I find verses 49–50 most interesting, especially where Jesus tells his parents he is here to do his Father's business and they do not understand. Why would they not understand? Didn't they know he was the Messiah and a divine messenger from God? Joseph knew from an angel in a dream (Matthew 1:18–24) and Mary knew from a visitation by the angel Gabriel (Luke 1:26–38). Do you now see how the Bible can be inconsistent?

Many religions seem to want an immaculate birth with no male intervention. Women were looked on as less than nothing at the time of Christ's birth. It seems women were elevated when it was useful to the patriarchs of society, and when they were not needed women were seen as unclean. If you want to look at it spiritually, it's always God's hand that brings us into being. We come into an earthly life when we need to perfect ourselves for God or, as in the case of Christ, we are on a mission for God.

The reason that Joseph is depicted as confused in the Bible is because he was so much older than Mary and he thought it wasn't possible for him to have children. Mary was only sixteen and he was close to forty, which in that day was very old. If you look at it in this light, we could all be conceived by God's immaculate hand to make sure we got here on earth to learn. If God wants to make it happen, it will happen. It's called divine intervention.

Look at Elizabeth, Mary's sister, who gave birth to John the Baptist at an age when women were supposedly past the reproductive age. John was born about six months before Christ and was his cousin and eventually became the great prophet and baptizer who was the "voice crying in the desert." John also foretold that Christ was the true messenger and Messiah. Both Christ's and John's families were prominent in the community because of their royal lineage, and many saw John as the possible Messiah.

Christ was born in the month of June, according to Francine. Early Christians had noted his birthday at various times, including during the months of May and April. The early Church fathers finally settled on December 25 because this was the high holy day for the Romans celebrating their sun god and it was their winter solstice (ours is December 21). Romans celebrated this holiday as a time of rebirth and renewal, so the Church, as they have in so many instances, took a pagan holiday and Christianized it. This is but one example that shows how the Church changed dates and times and facts to fit into their own political and moneymaking agendas; but we will get more into that later.

The Bible also tells us of the visit of the Magi at his birth and of the star of Bethlehem and angels visiting the shepherds proclaiming his birth. Again, Matthew and Luke give us these stories about his birth while Mark and John are silent on the matter. In the Gospel of Matthew we learn of the Magi, or three wise men, who come from the East following a star and arrive at the court of King Herod and ask, *"Where is he that is born king of the Jews? For we have seen his star in the east, and are come to adore him"* (Matthew 2:2). Now, Herod was upset about this news because he was the king of the Jews and didn't want any usurpers running around taking his crown. He tells the wise men to go find this child and come back to him with his whereabouts so that he can also adore him; but as we all know he intends to dispose of the child so that his supremacy is not threatened. The wise men go from the court of Herod and, following the star, come to Bethlehem (to fulfill a prophecy), where they find the Christ child and adore him and give him frankincense, gold and myrrh. We then are told that the wise men and Joseph both got messages in their sleep—the wise men to not return to Herod, and Joseph to flee to Egypt because Herod would kill Jesus if he didn't. According to Matthew, Joseph and Mary take the child and flee to Egypt.

Now, here again we run into inconsistency in the Bible. In the Gospel of Luke, Joseph and Mary take the child to the temple to be blessed and sanctified and then return to

Nazareth. In the Gospel of Matthew, the three of them flee to Egypt in fear of Herod's anger. They can't be in two places at the same time, so which one is right? Not only that, but if they did take the baby Jesus to the temple, would not Herod know of it, especially since he was looking for the child? Luke says that after the temple purification they returned to the city of Nazareth in Galilee and Christ grew up, making no mention of going to Egypt to hide from Herod. Now, since Herod did not die until almost four years later, why didn't Luke even mention the fact that Herod was a danger to the child Jesus? Was this story of Matthew a complete fabrication of the facts so that prophecy could be manipulated to apply to Christ? Many scholars think so.

Matthew specifically states that Herod killed all the male children who were two years of age and under in Bethlehem in the hope of destroying the newly born "king of the Jews" (Matthew 2:16). This act supposedly fulfilled another prophecy. Matthew then states an angel came to Joseph in a dream while he was in Egypt hiding and told him to go back to Israel (to fulfill another prophecy) because Herod was now dead. He then takes Mary and Christ to Nazareth (to fulfill yet another prophecy), where Christ grows up. Now, it seems clear here that the Gospel of Matthew was written with the obvious intent to fulfill Jewish prophecy as far as the Messiah is concerned, for it states each prophecy as it occurred. The Gospel of Luke does not do this and is a much more peaceful narrative.

Luke does not mention the star of Bethlehem or the wise men present at Christ's birth, only the shepherds to whom angels appeared to announce Christ's birth with a heavenly light. Matthew does not say anything about angels proclaiming the birth to shepherds (perhaps because there was no prophecy concerning angels proclaiming his birth). These two distinct accounts about Christ's birth and the several years after come into conflict with each other, especially as to the role of Herod and the danger to Christ. It seems probable that if King Herod had wanted Jesus dead, he could have killed him at any time during his first four years. The city of Nazareth was about sixty-five miles from Jerusalem while Bethlehem was very close to Jerusalem, so either was within easy distance of Herod's reach.

As you will see, this is perhaps the first of many

conflicting accounts of Christ in the New Testament. It is these conflicts that create the possibility of untruth and downright fabrication that Biblical scholars are constantly pointing out. Can we trust these biblical accounts when they seemingly give different versions that go against each other? Scholars who defend the Bible will constantly use the argument of "omission" in their defense. In this case they might say that Luke just omitted the part about Herod and Joseph and Mary fleeing to Egypt. These types of arguments strain our credulity because the "omission" is so important and significant.

Francine says that the Gospel of Luke is fairly accurate and that in this section of Matthew there is indeed fabrication for the sake of prophecy. In other words, whoever wrote this portion of the Gospel of Matthew completely made up the story about Herod and the flight to Egypt. She says there are parts of both accounts that are incorrect, but that Luke's account follows what actually happened more accurately. She states that there was a supernova in the sky at the time of his birth and that many came to adore and give homage and gifts to the Christ child—almost like a modern-day baby shower. The three

Magi, she states, were actually three wealthy merchants from the surrounding area and there were no angels proclaiming his birth to shepherds. She also relates that Christ was indeed taken to the temple to be blessed and sanctified according to Jewish law and custom.

The childhood of Jesus is addressed very little in the gospels. The Gospel of Luke gives us one account of Christ teaching in the temple at the age of twelve, but that is all that is related by any of the gospels. The story of Jesus teaching in the temple confirms what I wrote earlier and is another example of how Jesus's contemporaries viewed him and held him in an exalted state. Do you suppose that a little ragtag boy would be allowed in the temple to even listen to the elders there, not to mention actually teaching them? Of course not, but Christ was of royal lineage and came from a wealthy family and would have been treated with some deference and allowed into the temple. When, as I related earlier, his parents found him and he told them that "I must be about my father's business," they did not understand. But it shows that Christ knew in some way that he was going to be a leader and teacher of men. You must realize these were the elders, the theologians of the

Sanhedrin (lawmakers of Israel), and that they were held in rapt attention listening to a boy of royal heritage teaching them. Any other boy would have been viewed as an unruly, ostentatious, poor beggar kid who would have been thrown out of the holy council. They couldn't and wouldn't have thrown out a child of royal blood.

Even then he was trying to give the real truth to the Sanhedrin. The Gospel of Luke says he was twelve years old, but my guide says he was around ten years old when this incident took place. I don't think it's that important except it shows the infused knowledge that Jesus had and that he knew he was on a mission for God. This is so obvious in his aforementioned statement about his father's business. He meant, of course, God and not Joseph.

Before this incident in the temple, Jesus was like a normal Jewish boy who helped his father by working in a large compound for making furniture. As a child he would play with his brothers and two sisters and other friends and relatives like his cousin John, who would later be the Baptist. Among the friends he played with was Mary Magdalene, whom he did know as a child because she was from another fairly wealthy family. Jesus and Magdalene were actually childhood sweethearts, even if it was puppy love at that age. I will address later how Mary Magdalene became confused with Mary of Bethany and was branded a harlot.

There was an awful story that circulated for a time that Jesus shot birds with a slingshot for fun. This isn't even reasonable for an entity created by God as a direct report. Francine says that a bird he found was in bad shape with a broken wing and he healed it. This was the first time he used his healing powers. Francine also says as a boy he healed a rabid dog. This didn't seem to surprise anyone, because they all knew by infusion or observance that this was a child blessed by God.

As Jesus grew up he was allowed to have tutors and went many times to the temple to learn Jewish ritual law and the Hebrew language; but he, as well as most people in the area, spoke and wrote in the Aramaic language. As Jesus became more educated, not only in Jewish laws and traditions by his visits to the temple, but also in other subjects and philosophies by his tutors, he became more and more restless. Although he helped his father in his furniture business and was learning the skills of carpentry and furniture making, he knew he was destined for more.

Francine says that between the ages of fourteen and fif-teen, he told his parents that he wanted to travel and study other countries and their religions. Both Mary and Joseph were not thrilled with this idea, but Jesus insisted that it was necessary for what he had to do. They reluctantly agreed and sent him with two household workers and two of his brothers, James and John, and gave him a good sup-ply of money. In that day, it was not unusual for young teenagers to take on the responsibilities of adulthood. Women were often married at a young age and started having children because life spans were so short. Boys quickly became men and started working to help support their families, or even started their own families.

Thus we have the end of the childhood phase of Christ's life, and Jesus would now enter into a period of traveling and learning in preparation for what was to come. This period has long been termed "the lost years of Jesus," but it was to be perhaps the most gratifying and happy period of his life. These were the years in which he learned his great back-ground of wisdom and philosophy that he would put forth in his teachings, which, as we all know, changed the world.

CHAPTER 2

The Lost Years of Jesus

C AN YOU IMAGINE how frightening it must have been for Jesus at the age of fourteen or fifteen years old to leave his home and go out to explore the world? Frightening and exhilarating in that he could now expand his horizons beyond the towns of Nazareth and Bethlehem and the city of Jerusalem. No longer would he be mired in the everyday boredom of a small town such as Nazareth, doing work that he knew was not for him in his father's furniture business. He was off on a great adventure and knew inside that he had to learn and gather as much information as possible from the many cultures and people that he would meet along the way.

Before we get into the actual travels of Jesus, though, let's discuss something that really has not been discussed by theologians or scholars regarding Christ—that is, the whole premise of his having psychic abilities. Don't you find it interesting that no one in the world of academia or theology has really brought up this idea? Whether it is because they feel they will be ridiculed by their colleagues or whether, in the case of theologians, they will be deemed heretics, it really doesn't matter, the fact is that no one has ever really addressed it and just common sense makes it blatantly clear that Christ had to have some, if not many, psychic abilities or talents.

Since I myself am psychic, perhaps I can recognize the outward appearances of psychic ability more than most. It is perfectly clear to me that Christ manifested psychic powers. Maybe scholars and theologians either don't recognize these manifestations of psychic abilities or are afraid to make any conclusions about them, and therefore never bring them up in their studies. But the fact remains that there is overwhelming evidence in the writings about Jesus that he had psychic ability.

First of all, the actions of Christ in his life would indicate emphatically that he had to have had some sort of communication with God. Francine says that he was clairaudient and was able to hear and speak with God directly and that God first contacted him when he was four years old. (Now, skeptics out there might say something to the effect that here we go again, and if Christ heard a voice he was probably schizophrenic). It is interesting that scholars and theologians have no problem with the seemingly endless parade of prophets who bring the word of God throughout the Old Testament. These prophets are even quoted extensively in New Testament gospels like Matthew. Do we question how these prophets got their information from God? No, we do not; we just accept these prophets as part of history and *assume* their information came from God.

Just what constitutes a prophet? A prophet is a person who foretells future events or gives messages from a divinity. In modern-day terminology, he or she would be a clairvoyant, a psychic, a medium or clairaudient. Soothsayers, seers and oracles would all come under the definition of being prophets because they foretold future events. Religious figures such as Buddha or Muhammad would also be called prophets, for they brought messages from a higher power or divinity.

To call Jesus Christ a prophet would not be wrong, for he foretold future events such as his Passion; but in reality, he was more of a psychic and teacher. He healed many with his psychic abilities of healing by the laying on of hands, and his miracles of healing are told in many places of the New Testament. We also know that he was clairaudient, not only by his actions, but we also know of his conversation with God in the garden of Gethsemane, in which he asked God to lift the burden of his Passion. God must have replied because Christ said, "Thy will be done." So far we have Christ manifesting at least three different psychic abilities—clairvoyance (foreseeing the future), healing and clairaudience (hearing God).

We also hear of Christ walking on water, calming the sea in a storm, making a few fishes and pieces of bread into many, congregating fish for nets, making wine from water, raising the dead, and a multitude of other miracles. There are certainly some physical psychic abilities working here, where he can evidently manipulate the physical attributes of nature and the molecular structure of matter.

If, as the Bible says, these miracles attributed to Jesus took place, then we have a being who not only manifested psychic abilities like no other in history, but one who would seem to be empowered by our divine Creator to help him in his mission. The only problem that we seem to have doesn't come from Jesus, but from the works and manipulations of man, because as we have already asked—can we trust the accounts of the Bible?

I find it somewhat ironic that the very people (early Christians) who want the world to believe in the divinity of Christ are also the ones who threaten that divinity more than anyone else with their editing, manipulation and omissions of New Testament scripture that raise doubts as to its authenticity and truth. This is then compounded with a Church that has perhaps one of the most bloody and corrupt histories known to man in its search and implementation for power and control. I know I have said this several times, but if Christ came down to earth in this day and age, I don't believe he would want to call himself a Christian. It is a sad commentary for our wonderful Messiah.

* * *

Christ and his small entourage joined a trade caravan and set off first for the area we know as Turkey today. As an aside, when I visited Turkey I found that the Turkish people will fight you if you deny Jesus' trip to Ankara, where he eventually passed through again later on in life. I found Ankara to be a very holy place, more holy than most churches I've been to because Jesus had been there. The Turkish Christians also fully believe in the Anatola (the Mother God), and even their rugs show her in symbolism with her hands on her hips.

Jesus studied in Turkey at Byzantium (later known as Constantinople and today as Istanbul), its capital city. This was a meeting place of scholars, merchants, artisans and theologians, and this is where he was first introduced to various beliefs in Gnosticism. As he preached, Christ was a seeker of knowledge and wisdom and he avidly learned as many philosophies as possible from his travels. Francine says he stayed in a type of villa, using money from the family coffers. The picture of a poor, beggarly man—dusty and dirty—is just not factual. He wore fine garments and traveled with well-kept family and assistants. He ate at the best tables and studied with Persian and Arab scholars. He had a photographic mind and assimilated everything. While in Byzantium he became friends with a scribe who took down his thoughts and musings.

Francine says that Jesus stayed in Byzantium only a few months, but even then he seemed to gather crowds of people around him. You must realize that in Eastern countries they are used to holy people or prophets who come and go, especially if they are on their own journey or mission. Many fakirs (holy men) even today travel in India by delivering wisdom and then go on to village after village living off alms given them. Jesus attracted people because of his charisma and innate wisdom and even though he was still very young, he always seemed to make an impression on those around him.

His search for knowledge, combined with the exuberance of youth, spurred him onward toward the Far East. Francine says he left Byzantine and traveled eastward through the Anatolia region of Turkey, where he assimilated philosophy about the Mother God and then continued onward southeast into what was then known as Mesopotamia (Iraq) and the city of Babylon. From Babylon he went into what was then known as Persia (Iran) and eastward through Afghanistan into ancient India. Having money, he secured passages on trade caravans for protection and the best routes to India.

Francine says he stayed in India for close to ten years, studying under the Brahmans of the Hindu religion and also under Buddhist priests. While in India, he traveled to the areas of Kashmir and Tibet, seeking the highest teachers and masters possible for his studies. After some years, he sent his brothers back home to Israel with messages for his parents that he would be studying for an extended period of time. They put up a great resistance because James, who was very close to him and a sensitive in his own right, knew with all certainty that Christ's road would be fraught with pain and suffering and skepticism. Jesus more or less convinced them that they had to go back because his mission had to be done and was written in the scriptures, and also convinced them that they were needed at home and could help him more there by taking care of the family. So James and John and their servants went back to Israel, knowing that Jesus was staying on to study and prepare for what he had to do.

Francine says that while James was with Jesus, he did

take notes and did to a certain degree document their travels with a journal or diary. She also says that sometime in the not too distant future, some or all of these writings will be discovered by archaeologists, much as the National Geographic Society recently found the Gospel of Judas.

Francine says Jesus was attracted to these Eastern philosophies because of their simple wisdoms and teachings of peace and that his brothers were more inclined to be skeptical because they had been ingrained with the ideas of Jewish rebellion against the Romans. As history tells us, later on these differences were made apparent when James and John became members of the Jewish Christians and James became their head, but we will get into that later in the book.

While in India and the surrounding areas, Christ again started attracting followers. According to Francine, he had several disciples while in India and crowds would gather to listen to this young but seemingly wise man from Israel. It is also at this time that Jesus became much more ascetic in his way of life to concentrate on his studies. He mingled with the poor and even did some healings.

Unlike the Bible that states Jesus' first miracle was at the wedding feast of Cana (when he turned water into wine), Francine says his first miracle was when he healed a boy of leprosy in the area of what is now known as Calcutta in India. This was not a startling revelation to a country both then and now used to seeing a prophet or holy man able to levitate, heal and give spiritual knowledge. Many of the holy men in India had done such acts. Francine says he was directed by God to do this, as it was a sort of baptism by fire for what was to come.

As he studied and learned, his old Judaic teachings of a vengeful and fearful God changed to that of a loving and compassionate God. Although the more passive religions of Hinduism and Buddhism attracted him, Jesus could not reconcile his total belief in one true God with all of their teachings. He did embrace the philosophy of reincarnation and also the many loving concepts of both religions. He also learned to communicate on the level of his audience . . . giving stories and parables to get his message across to the poor and illiterate, rather than preaching dogma that they could not understand. This wisdom was to serve him for the rest of his days.

For those of you who think this is pure fantasy, I have a big surprise in store for you. There are dozens of texts from Eastern scholars that indicate that Christ was indeed in India and the surrounding areas at that time. He was called by many names by different cultures of people—"Issa," "Isa," "Yuz Asaf," "Budasaf," "Yuz Asaph," "San Issa" and "Yesu." Many of these texts point out that he was a prophet or holy man from another land and some even point out that he was from Israel.

In Kashmir, in the city of Srinagar, are two separate fascinating monuments. First, there is the Roza Bal (or Razabal), which is purported to be the tomb of Jesus Christ. According to the beliefs of those in the area, Christ came to this area after his survival of the crucifixion and lived to be 120 years of age and was then buried in this tomb. Also, on a large hill of the city called the Takhat Sulaiman (Throne of Solomon), there is a monument that has four inscriptions, two of which are still legible. The inscriptions were recorded, however, and read as follows:

The mason of this pillar is Bihishti Zargar. Year fifty and four.

Khwaja Rukun son of Murjan erected this pillar.

At this time Yuz Asaf proclaimed his prophethood. Year fifty and four.

He is Jesus, Prophet of the Children of Israel.

Now, these monuments are very perplexing to Christians. They logically relate to Christ coming back to this area after his survival of the crucifixion. Therein lies the problem, because the Christian faith believes Christ died on the cross. One of the monuments is even supposed to be his tomb! (Francine says that the tomb doesn't contain his body, because he actually died in France, but the people of the area so venerated him that they put up a symbolic tomb). Here we have two monuments in the obscure area of Kashmir that say categorically that Christ not only survived the crucifixion, but also came to this area after that event and lived. Both of these monuments are very ancient and date to the time of Christ, but are we to readily surmise that they are some elaborate hoax? What in God's name would be the point of creating such an ornate fake when it is believed that Christ wasn't even known outside of Israel yet? It was not for several hundred years after his supposed death that Christianity would even become a popular religion. Christian scholars cannot give a reasonable explanation for these monuments, while scholars who believe he did go to India say they are part of their proof that he did, and still other scholars who believed he survived the crucifixion also say this is proof of his survival.

Although the evidence seems to be substantial, it is not the only evidence that is out there concerning Jesus' travels. There are many Eastern texts that mention him and his works in the Far East. It is also interesting to note that one of the largest religions in the world, Islam, venerates Christ as a prophet and messenger from God. Muslims believe he survived the crucifixion and did not die on the cross. I certainly cannot relate all the sources here, for they are too many, but if you would like to read more about this time in Christ's life, you can start by reading the following books: *The Jesus Mystery* by Janet Brock; *Jesus Lived in India* by Holger Kersten; *The Unknown Life of Jesus Christ* by Nicholas Notovich; and *A Search for the Historical Jesus* by Dr. Fida Hassnain.

Let's be logical about this. Why would these Far Eastern texts reference Jesus and praise and talk about this wonderful prophet and teacher from Israel and the Holy Land if they had never seen him? Why would they make up a fictional character like this? The religion of Islam was not in existence yet, so there was no agenda to promote it or to try to downplay the divinity of Christ. The faith of Christianity was just starting and didn't have any scope or influence whatsoever at that time; and Hinduism and Buddhism were pacifistic religions confined to the Far East. Pure logic just dictates that there was no hoax or fiction and that these writings were true.

These ancient texts of the Far East haven't been ignored by scholars, but they have been suppressed and/or ignored by many Christian scholars and the Church. Why, you might ask? To perpetuate the dogma that the Catholic Church and other Christian churches have put out for centuries. Can you imagine how the truth about Christ's surviving the crucifixion and not ascending into heaven but living on in other countries would rock Christianity? The Christian world would be devastated, not because it in any way affects the divinity of Christ, but because their Church had covered up the truth.

Just as the Church has suppressed its influence on the makeup of the New Testament, so it seems to extend to the life of Christ and how he lived and died. As we progress through Christ's life, you will see the glaring holes of untruth about him, perpetuated by the Church, surfacing time and time again. Much of this can be blamed on Paul, the self-proclaimed apostle, and the Church adopting "Pauline Christianity." Although Paul never met Christ and was never an eyewitness to any portion of his life, we have Paul "interpreting" what Christ meant and how he lived his life. It is Paul who says Christ ascended into heaven (backed up by Church editing of gospels), and it is Paul who brings forth the whole concept of atonement (dying for our sins). Christ said nothing about atonement, but Paul put it forth to the masses as his own interpretation and it has become a weapon for guilt ever since. In my humble opinion, the Catholic Church's biggest error was in following Paul's lead. Big mistake.

Another aspect of the character of Jesus, according to

my guide, Francine, is the fact that he was basically a loner at this time in his life. Even though he loved his mother, through his parables he talks more of the father figure. Jesus was ever the prodigal son because of his devotion to God the Father. Loving his Father in heaven at the age of fourteen or fifteen probably was the very thing that set him on his journey. Some authors feel that Jesus, who was the eldest child, abandoned his mother so he could travel after his father, Joseph, died. I don't feel this is true. Mary apparently had enough money and the other brothers carried on the work. He wouldn't have been much of a spiritual messiah if he left his mother a destitute widow.

Through his parables he shows that he did have sympathy for the poor widow. He even speaks of a mother who lost a silver coin and lit a lamp and swept all night until she found it. Some theologians feel this was his guilt coming out for having left his mother. I don't see it this way, not only because he gives examples of poverty, widowhood, how to trust your servants, etc., in his teachings, but also that he was just giving a view on the poverty that did exist at the time. The father figure psychologically plays out favorably by Jesus feeling more comfortable being surrounded by men. But that could also be because women did not have the status of men at that time. Even though Christ is known to have given women a more equal status with men, if you look closely most of the healings in the Bible attributed to him were of men. Now, in no way do I want to portray Jesus as a misogynist who was disrespectful of women, but custom in those times dictated that women were not treated as equals to men. He was raised in a culture of unequal status between male and female, but he defended them and softened toward women as he got older.

I think this traveling period of aloneness was filled with anguish and sometimes despair. I have always believed— call it intuition or my psychic ability—that he knew what was in store for him later on in his life. To know that he was the Messiah or the chosen one would have been frightening to anyone. This time of traveling and learning in other countries was really a dichotomy to him because on the one hand he was happy in the learning of new philosophies, religions and cultures; and yet, on the other hand, he had this weight of being the Messiah constantly on his shoulders.

The internal strife within him must have been difficult to bear. Two factions were operating—the fear of what was to come on the emotional side and yet the intellect knew what he had to do and what his destiny was. I'm sure no other living person knew his Chart like he did. Most of us just blindly live life and hope we are spiritually on track. I'm also sure the human part of him rebelled against his fate, but he knew it was written and this heavy responsibility must have weighed heavily on him. So, being the Messiah, he had to avail himself of all possible learning—not only in the synagogue but in the local areas of Galilee, Nazareth, Bethlehem and other local towns; as well as other countries and cultures with their philosophies and religions. He had to be astute about people and the social and political climate, as well as the economic patterns of the times, and yet knowing that things and people don't change much. That's why his parables are timeless. People don't change much, just their time and topography. People still cheat, treat each other badly, waste their money and look down on the poor and lower classes. He knew he had to learn and talk for the ages. Truth is truth and it is immutable and it doesn't matter if it's spoken now or two thousand years ago.

In the book *The Passover Plot* by Hugh J. Schonfield, the author agrees with some of this, especially Christ's love of his heavenly Father. But the author and I disagree on his seeming neglect of his mother. We truly don't hear much about her, but we certainly don't hear anything about Joseph. I'm sure he got his information about life outside his home because he left so young. Jesus was obviously a great observer, and from the observance of others in family life or just the conclusions he came to by watching others through his journeys, he had a great insight into how people reacted to one another.

I myself, not just through research, but in dealing with probably millions of people in fifty-three years of being a psychic and doing lectures and twenty readings a day, have found that you can't help but start forming a true statistical analysis over time. Even in more than half a century I've seen that there are still the same concerns and problems and worries that have always been and will be until the end of time.

At the age of twenty-five or twenty-six years old, Jesus left India and traveled to Egypt. While there, he studied the ancient Egyptian and Persian mysteries and more

Gnostic teachings. After about a year, he then traveled to Qumran and lived and studied with the Essenes for a while. It was also at this time that he resumed his relationship with Mary Magdalene, whom he had kept in touch with by letters. While with the Essenes, he adopted a great deal of their philosophy, and although he didn't subscribe to the very conservative and ascetic facets, he did relate to members of the Essene sect who were a bit more liberal, and they considered him one of them. The Essenes are thought to have lived solely in the area of Qumran, but recent archaeological discoveries have also indicated that they had a complex on Mount Sion in Jerusalem and in several other areas. The Essenes were very private and didn't allow many outsiders into their communities. We will see later how Christ moved freely within these Essene communities, and that was because he was accepted as an Essene.

Perhaps one of the greatest testaments that you could give to Christ was the fact that even though he knew his destiny, he never wavered from it. In *The Passover Plot,* Schonfield states: "Whatever Jesus learned, however, and in whatever way he obtained his knowledge, including elements of the healing art cultivated and practiced by the communities of 'the Saints' [a group attached to the Essenes], there was always before him the destiny for which he prepared. In the last resort, he alone, earnestly soliciting the help of the Heavenly Father, must penetrate to the inner recesses of the sacred writings and marshal in order the intimations of the Divine Oracles. The novel achievement of Jesus was to mark out clearly the path the Messiah would have to tread. *Thus it was written.*"

This really helps substantiate what Francine said more than thirty years ago: Jesus not only was a gatherer of knowledge, but also put it into reasonable terms and language understandable to an illiterate group of people. Instead of preaching Judaic law and theology like the priests in the Temple, he would talk to the people in parables and stories that they could understand and use in everyday life.

Many scholars and laypeople ask the inevitable questions: Who was Jesus really? What was he really about? Was he the son of God or the son of man? I feel that the confusion lies in what is referred to as "Christology." Most Christians believe that Jesus is simultaneously the Son of God and also God made flesh.

Most other religions also venerate Jesus in varying

degrees. Eastern religions like Hinduism and Buddhism recognize him as a prophet, and as stated earlier, Islam considers him to be one of God's most beloved and important prophets. Muslims do not accept the divinity of Christ or the crucifixion—saying either it didn't happen or that Jesus did not die on the cross.

Francine says Jesus was a special entity who had a Chart as a messenger to bring mankind to a true picture of our Divinity as an all-loving God. She doesn't discredit Buddha or Muhammad, but just states he was a direct report or creation from God. She has always stated that we all are sons and daughters of God, but Jesus was created for a special purpose.

There has never been as much controversy over a figure such as our Lord, and probably never will be. You don't see theologians in any other culture fighting and obsessing and researching any of the other messengers as they do with Jesus. This is because the Christian Church from the beginning was so flawed. So many Christian factions with their own interpretations did so much infighting that it caused schisms that have not been repaired to this day. The New Testament and the Bible were not put together until almost three hundred years after Christ's supposed death and crucifixion, and experts say that at least twenty-seven, and in some cases some claim over forty, books were not included that should have been. Who did the picking and choosing of what should be in the Bible and what should not? The early Christian Church.

Before we can understand the works, life and individual known as Jesus Christ, we first have to understand the sources from which the information comes about him. If someone tells you a story about something or someone, do you not want to know if the story is true? Do you not want to verify the truth and consistency of the information given in the story? Science certainly does. It's called proof. If you don't ask for proof, you are basically accepting hearsay and trusting that the teller of the story is in actuality telling the truth. It is here that we run into a big problem, for man and his penchant for embellishment and fabrication and downright lies comes into play. Let me try to explain this logically and objectively.

Try to picture yourself in the time of the early Christian Church. We have this fledgling religion that is essentially being put forth by word of mouth by twelve apostles and a few others. They travel to areas of Judaea and different lands and countries and preach the words of Jesus Christ. As converts to the new religion take place, its members quickly become a mixture of different races, ethnic groups and cultures with various backgrounds of other religions in existence at the time. The early Church soon finds itself divided into several main factions . . . the "Pauline Christians," who follow the teachings of Paul, the self-proclaimed apostle who never met or was eyewitness to any part of Christ's life; the "Jewish Christians," who follow the teachings and leadership of Christ's brother James; the "Gnostic Christians," who combine Christianity with the theories of gnosis (mainly from Egypt and Persia); and lastly, other Christians who follow the basic teachings of Peter and some other disciples, and who are quickly assimilated into the faction of Pauline Christians after the death of Peter.

These factions are almost immediately at odds with each other. Pauline Christians hold firm to their pronounced beliefs that Jesus was divine and the son of God incarnate, that he died on the cross for our sins, and that forty days after his crucifixion he ascended into heaven. Jewish Christians, who included many of Christ's relatives, were led by James, had their headquarters in Jerusalem and held firm in their beliefs that Jesus was not a divine son of God but a messenger or prophet from God, and that belief is because he survived the crucifixion and died a natural death later (who would know the truth about his death if not his relatives?). They also firmly still believed in Judaic laws and customs and integrated Christ's teachings into their Judaic teachings. Gnostic Christians believed in the divinity of Jesus as a special messenger from God and that his teachings were divine. They also believed that he did not die on the cross, and they did not believe in the ascension. They did not subscribe to Judaic laws and teachings and instead utilized Christ's teachings to augment those of gnosis and the ancient mysteries.

The battle was on for control of the early Christian Church and would last for several centuries. The outcome was a foregone conclusion, however, for several reasons. Pauline Christianity had its seat of power in Rome and was greatly influenced by Roman domination of the world at the time. Jewish Christianity had its power in Jerusalem and was greatly influenced by Judaism and the occupation of Israel by Rome. Gnostic Christians had no real power base, were mainly in Egypt and Persia, and reached only to a limited number of people because their teachings appealed mainly to scholars and learned men.

In the first few years of Christianity, the Christians in Rome (Pauline Christians) were persecuted severely, while the Jewish Christians in Jerusalem were allowed to build a church. Gnostic Christians basically kept to themselves or went underground. Over the next several hundred years, Pauline Christians, while still being persecuted, were starting to cooperate more with the ruling Romans. Jewish Christians, however, due to several Jewish rebellions, were almost completely wiped out by the Romans and had their church and Temple destroyed. Gnostic Christians were making some headway, with Egyptian Coptic Churches being formed as their philosophy of gnosis spread, but were too few in number to have any impact otherwise.

Finally, at the Council of Nicaea in 325 A.D., the Roman emperor Constantine made Pauline Christianity the state religion of Rome and it became the Roman Catholic Church. This act was highly important and significant, because it paved the way for Christianity as we know it today and also the Bible as we know it today.

Each faction of the early Christians had their favorite writings or what they considered to be canonical texts on the life of Jesus Christ. By winning the war, so to speak, the Pauline Christians were able to formulate and adopt their favorite writings and then put them together by editing, adding, deleting and omitting any texts that were favored by the other factions. The Bible is certainly without numerous texts that deserve to be in it. Early Pauline Christians edited it for their own purposes and agendas. Later on in history, the formation of the Anglican Church in England caused the Bible to be edited even more and the result was the "King James" version of the Bible.

Almost every serious biblical scholar acknowledges the fact that the Bible has been edited, copied, deleted from and added to by early Christians. How can we then trust the New Testament of the Bible as a legitimate source of truth about Jesus Christ? The answer is that we really can't trust it; but at this time it is one of our main sources of information about Christ because there are so few other sources available. Yes, we have some information from Gnostic texts that were discovered at Nag Hammadi in Egypt in 1945, the recent Gospel of Judas discovery, and some other texts like the Dead Sea Scrolls; but the information is limited and also is fighting for recognition against almost seventeen hundred years of traditional belief in the Bible.

With that in mind, as we delve more into Christ's life and works you will find me questioning certain aspects related about him in the Bible. I do this not to criticize the Bible so much as to point out discrepancies and possible errors in the four accepted gospels that don't give an accurate picture of Christ or his life. My writer's responsibility to give out truth far outweighs any consideration for "traditional beliefs" or historical untruths that have been perpetuated by religion for their own expedient reasons. For those who want to delve more into the history of how the Christian Bible was put together, I recommend the essay by Richard Carrier, "The Formation of the New Testament Canon." You can find it on the fairly controversial Web site—www. infidels.org. I really am just trying to give as clear and precise a picture as I can about Jesus Christ, his works, his mission and his life to my readers. It is then the readers' choice to do what they want to do with that information.

CHAPTER 3

His Baptism and Gathering of Disciples

J ESUS STUDIED WITH the Essenes for almost two years and related to them his travels and experiences in the Far East. He shared much of what he had learned in healing, meditation and Eastern philosophy. Being a secular sect, the Essenes did not travel extensively and much of the information and knowledge he gave them was new and exciting to most of them. The Essenes were Gnostic in many ways. They constantly debated new philosophies and ideas and were very adept at writing. The Dead Sea Scrolls were found in caves just outside of Qumran in 1947 and have been attributed to the Essenes.

Fifteen years of study was a lot of time to delve into how others believed and worshipped. This, I am sure, is also what gave him his caring and knowledge of the poor and downtrodden. Six months before his thirtieth birthday, Jesus made his way back to Nazareth. The time for his public life in Israel had come.

There was a great homecoming celebration for Jesus. He had been gone for so many years and had become such a wise and caring man. His mother, Mary, was there, as were all his brothers and sisters, and the guests included Mary Magdalene as well as many cousins that included Martha and aunts that included Mary Cleophas and Mary Salome. The Bible speaks of these relatives having Christ over for dinner and having long talks together. They really formed a close-knit family and community of friends and relatives who were always around Jesus. Many scholars think that up to five of his apostles were related to him. Jesus would relate many stories about his travels and experiences to them and they were always a rapt audience.

As an aside, I'm sure that many of the original books of the Bible contained much of this material. The reason we don't find it is because it was edited out by the early Church.

They wanted to control the minds of the people who read the Bible and wanted them to only read what they "deemed" was best for them. Anything that seemed to make Jesus more human or a seeker of knowledge must have made them feel he wasn't completely infused by God. How ignorant for one not to know that everything from every sector is infused by God. The early Church didn't want the populace to become scholars; they wanted followers who would blindly follow what they said. We never hear Christ say you have to follow any particular religion such as Judaism, Christianity or Hinduism. He was just a seeker of truth. His words of wisdom, "Seek and you shall find" and "Knock and it shall be opened to you," are very strong indications that his words were always a product of his learning and Gnostic philosophy. If he didn't want us to be free thinkers, he would have said so.

After reuniting with his mother and Mary Magdalene, he commenced his public life. The wedding feast at Cana was actually his wedding to Magdalene. The wedding, when read in the Bible (John 2:1–11), just seems to stick out, with no explanation except that this was supposedly his first miracle. When his mother comes to him and says

that the guests have no wine, he is reluctant to do anything. Mary, however, knowing Jewish custom, just orders
the servants to do whatever Jesus tells them to do without
saying another word to Jesus. He then evidently tells the
servants to bring six large jars of water, which he then
turns into wine, and instructs them to give it to the chief
guest (best man) of the feast.

We then read about the chief guest, after tasting the
wine, calling the bridegroom aside and saying (John 2:10),
*"Every man at first brings the best wine; and when they have
drunk, then that which is weak; but* you *have kept the best
wine until now."* Now, what is so significant about this?
Mary knew that the Jewish custom at weddings was that
the bridegroom was responsible for supplying the wine. So
who made the wine that was supplied to the guests? Christ
did, and it was he whom the best man called forth! I cannot understand why others have not seen this, other than
to ignore it because they didn't want anyone to think that
Jesus was married. That also explains why Mary was so
even-tempered about the situation and didn't bother to say
anything more to Jesus other than to notify him that wine
was needed. She knew that as the bridegroom, Jesus had to

supply the wine! To further substantiate this, Jesus from that time onward was called Rabbi, which can mean "teacher"; but was a title almost always conferred on a married man per Jewish custom.

Timelines in the Bible can be confusing, because the four gospels don't always agree to incidents happening at the same time (more inconsistency). For instance, right after Christ's wedding at Cana, the Gospel of John has Jesus going to Jerusalem and driving money changers out of the Temple. This incident is also mentioned in the other three gospels of Matthew, Mark and Luke, but they put this incident forth as happening later on in Christ's life. Francine says that the incident regarding the money changers did happen later on, so the Gospel of John is incorrect as to the time it occurred in Christ's life. Now, this may seem fairly insignificant to many, but if you are going to use the Bible as a factual text for proof, then you have to live with the consequences when it is shown to be blatantly incorrect as well. This also again shows that the Bible contains errors and cannot always be relied on as an absolute text.

The interesting thing about the Gospel of John is that it doesn't always follow the lead of the other three gospels.

Much of the Gospel of John relates incidents in Christ's life that the other three gospels don't mention, and conversely the Gospel of John doesn't mention many of the incidents in the other three gospels. Such seems to be the case in the next major incidents of Christ's life—his baptism and temptation in the wilderness.

The four gospels of Matthew, Mark, Luke and John all mention that Christ was baptized by John the Baptist and that John proclaimed the coming of the Messiah. John was Christ's cousin; however, it is only in the Gospel of Matthew that we even get a small clue to the fact that they knew each other. In Matthew 3:13–15 we read: *Then Jesus came from Galilee to the Jordan to John, to be baptized by him. But John tried to stop him, saying, I need to be baptized by you, and yet have you come to me? But Jesus answered and said to him, Permit it now, for this is necessary for us so that all righteousness may be fulfilled; and then he permitted him.* There definitely is an implication of intimacy here in the brief conversation between John and Jesus. The gospels of Mark and Luke just basically relate that John baptized Jesus. The Gospel of John does relate that John baptized Jesus, but also implies that John didn't know Christ. We read in John

1:29–34 the following: *The next day John saw Jesus coming to him, and he said, Behold the Lamb of God who takes away the sin of the world! This is the one of whom I said, The man who comes after me is yet ahead of me, because he was before me. And I did not know him; but that he might be made known to Israel, I came to baptize with water. And John testified, saying, I saw the Spirit descending from heaven like a dove, and it rested upon him. And yet I did not know him; but he who sent me to baptize with water said to me, The one upon whom you see the Spirit descending and resting, he is the one who will baptize with the Holy Spirit. And I saw and testified that this is the Son of God.*

This might seem to be another contradiction since John was Christ's cousin and boyhood playmate, but Francine gives a very good explanation. She says that Christ had not seen John for more than fifteen years and that John didn't recognize him as a man because he had last seen him as a boy. I also feel that this is very plausible, but in addition, I feel that the Gospel of John is also saying that even though John knew Jesus as his cousin, he didn't know he was the actual Messiah that both he and other prophets had foretold was coming. It was only when the Holy Spirit in the form of a dove descended on Jesus that John recognized that Jesus was indeed the chosen one of God. When he says, "I didn't know him," it is meant only in the aspect that he didn't know his cousin was the Messiah and seems somewhat shocked, which would bring out the second "I did not know him" in an almost incredulous manner.

Before we get into Christ's time in the wilderness, which is the next incident in his life as portrayed by most of the gospels, I want to relate what happened to John the Baptist. John was somewhat of a rabble-rouser. He spoke what he believed to be the truth and didn't care much about whom he offended. In my research, I've found that John the Baptist was also an Essene like Christ. It was the Jewish sect of Essenes that put forth the concept of baptism. They believed that baptism was to cleanse one of traumas and bad actions from past lives and not of original sin (but we'll get into that in a little bit). Unlike Christ, John subcribed to the strict and ascetic teachings of the Essenes. Francine says this is because John had spent his whole life in Roman-occupied Israel and, like a lot of Judaic men, resented the Romans. He was a revolutionist in his own thinking. While Jesus had been subjected to more passive and loving teachings, John had not. Following the strict asceticism of the Essenes, he preached to all who would listen and baptized thousands. It was his strict interpretation of Jewish law that eventually got him into trouble with Herod. Before that time, Herod and the hierarchy of the Temple viewed John as a dangerous nuisance because of his preaching against the hypocrisies of both of them.

John the Baptist would most probably have survived if he hadn't gone against Herodias, the wife of Herod. He called Herod and Herodias adulterers and Herodias a harlot because Herodias had divorced Herod's brother and married Herod while he was still alive. John's accusation angered Herodias and she used Herod's attraction for his stepdaughter Salome (fathered by Herod's brother previously) to gain her revenge. We all know the story about Herod becoming drunk and asking Salome to dance for him. She refuses and he begs her to dance and even promises anything up to half his kingdom to her for her dance. She asks her mother what she should demand and her mother says, "The head of John the Baptist." Salome then asks for his head and Herod, afraid to go back on his word, reluctantly has John executed and his head brought forth on a platter. Francine says when Jesus heard about his cousin John's death, he immediately sat down and cried in tremendous grief.

While the Essenes saw baptism as a washing-away of all past life traumas, Christianity made it into a cleansing of the sins of Adam and Eve (original sin). This, I feel, is a really bad interpretation. Most scholars believe that the story of Adam and Eve in Genesis of the Old Testament is symbolic in nature. The story of Adam and Eve reads like mythology and is meant to be symbolic. If read literally it doesn't make any sense, especially when it comes to the part about the sons of Adam and Eve marrying women and having wives and children. When Cain went to the land of Nod he got married, but where did his wife and the wife of his brother Seth come from? If it is read as a symbolic tale, however, the presence of these other people is only part of the symbolism and can be considered a valid extension of the story. The Tree of Knowledge is a tree whose fruit bears the knowledge of all good and evil. It is the symbol of knowledge, but it is also the symbol of temptation; and God tells both Adam and Eve that they can eat anything but the fruit of that tree.

Then there is the symbolism of the snake telling Eve it's all right to eat of the fruit of the Tree of Knowledge. The use of the snake was in rebuttal to all the fertility gods in the various pagan religions that surrounded Israel. When Solomon built the first Temple for Israel, its main columns were fashioned to represent snakes and fertility, as there was a lot of influence of other religions in ancient Israel. The snake thus represents symbolically these other religions tempting the people of Israel, who are represented symbolically by Adam and Eve—their supposed parents. Eve eats the fruit and also persuades Adam to eat the fruit. Women (represented by Eve) are forever branded as temptresses to men (represented by Adam)—even to this day. I've always said Adam got what he deserved—what kind of wimp was Adam that he went along with it? Adam and Eve then put on clothes to hide their nakedness. God looks for Adam, finds him, and Adam says he had hidden because he was naked. Then God asks, "Who told you that you were naked?"

This particular area of Genesis also brings up another inconsistency in the Bible, for it portrays God as not knowing everything when we all know he does. We find him asking, "Where are you, Adam?" as well as the question about his nakedness. God would know where Adam was and He would also know who tempted Eve, who tempted Adam, etc. Whenever you have the hand of man doing the writing, you will always find error and inconsistency.

The whole story of Adam and Eve is the symbolic story of humankind leaving paradise (the Other Side) and coming down to incarnate on the negative plane of Earth. Evil does not exist on the Other Side (or paradise), so Adam and Eve were banished to the Earth "to till the fields for their food" and "to bear their children in pain." This is pure symbolism at its finest and does teach that the Earth plane is negative and full of temptation and evil. Think of this, how do you learn unless you go to a negative plane where evil and temptation exist to test the mettle of your soul? You can't learn about evil in a perfect environment, but as evil is part of knowledge you must learn about it so that you know what good is. To learn about evil does not make you evil, it just gives you the knowledge to avoid becoming evil.

Thus, the concept of "original sin" was born in the symbolism of Adam and Eve eating the fruit of the tree that God told them not to eat. We can thereby deduce that if the story about original sin is symbolic, then so is the concept. "Original Sin" is just symbolic of the fact that although God is perfect, His/Her creations are not and are always in the state of being tempted on this plane we call Earth.

We then have three of the gospels—Matthew, Mark and Luke—relating how Christ was taken into the wilderness. John is silent on this incident. According to the gospels that relate it, Jesus was "taken" by the Holy Spirit to the wilderness after the heavens opened and a voice said, "You are my beloved son; with you I am pleased." They go on to relate how Christ fasted for forty days and nights and how the "adversary" (edited in as Satan) tempted Jesus by promising him riches and fame. Mark is very short on this, while both Matthew and Luke go into dialogues between Jesus and the adversary.

Francine disagrees with their account because she says he went to the desert after about a year in public life. He went alone as he wanted to contemplate and be free to hear God's voice. He knew what lay ahead and wanted to steel himself against it. Francine says that no devil as such came and tempted him, but he did do battle with his own conscience. He knew with his charisma he could have been an august ruler by socializing with the Sanhedrin and politicians and giving in to the mores of that day. He would have had wealth and the power to go with it. This was a time of quiet meditation and retrospection in which he communicated with his Father in heaven in preparation for what he had to do. While Matthew and Luke relate conversations with the adversary, Francine says that these conversations were made up to reflect the ever-increasing belief of the early Church in an entity called the devil. Francine says it may make for a good story, but simply isn't true; and after thirty (not forty) days in which he only at times fasted and at other times ate some food and had drink, he came out to rejoin his family.

Mary Magdalene, according to Francine, was always by his side and some teachings in Gnostic beliefs put forth that she was the direct report of the Mother God at that time, known as Sophia, just as Christ was a direct report of God the Father. They were here as replications of the true Mother and Father God. We all have within us the DNA of the divine Creators; but Mary and Jesus were examples of life as it should be lived, how marriage should be upheld and how love of humankind should be primary.

The Knights Templar, later on, seemed to believe this and tried to protect this knowledge and were murdered for it; although many escaped with knowledge of the information and what Christ's heritage was.

Christ then sets on his path to pick men who will follow him and become disciples. For the sake of continuity and understanding, I will always try to follow the timeline that the majority of gospels put forth. Where there is a discrepancy, I will point it out if it is of a significant nature. We will find that most of these discrepancies will have the Gospel of John right in the middle of them, but other books clash, too, as we have already noticed with the gospels of Matthew and Luke. I personally like the Gospel of John, but as you will continue to see, his gospel is much different than the others in many respects.

As John does not mention Christ's time in the wilderness, John has Christ gathering disciples immediately (Chapter 1) while Luke, Mark and Matthew have him getting his disciples after his time in the desert. There is some discrepancy in the gospels about whom Jesus gathered first as his disciple. John says Andrew and another who remained unidentified. Luke, Mark and Matthew have Jesus calling on both Simon (Peter) and Andrew, who were brothers and fishermen, and then James and John (also brothers and fishermen). Some of the gospels go on to tell about Jesus picking up other disciples, and not always in the same order, but I really think this is of little consequence. I'm only trying to make you realize the scope of the inconsistencies that are throughout the New Testament.

Jesus initially picked twelve disciples. They included Simon (Peter); Andrew the brother of Simon (Peter); James the son of Zebedee; John the brother of James of Zebedee; Levi (Matthew); Philip; Bartholomew; Thomas; James the son of Alpheus; Simon who was called Zelotes (and also known as Simon the Zealot or Simon the Canaanite); Jude (also known as Judas, son of James and Labbaeus); and Judas Iscariot. With two Simons and two Jameses and two Judases among his disciples, they often can get confused. Jesus wanted men he could teach and, in following him, obey orders. He knew what he was going to teach them had to be shared with the world by men who would spread out and give the knowledge to the many peoples in different lands.

He had people from all walks of life as his disciples, from Matthew the tax collector to the fishermen Peter, Andrew, James and John. He picked from the rich and the poor so he could get a wide swatch from every facet of life. This was clever, because it shows much thought went into whom he picked and why. It really was very astute, and let's even use the word prophetic, to realize his public life would be short, so he had to have men who would follow, listen and spread the word long after he had ceased to be around. He could have picked scholars, but they might have already been indoctrinated. It was better to get a so-called blank slate than to fight men who had their philosophies of life already strongly in place.

Some went ahead from village to village to proclaim the coming of this prophet who would give them truth and perhaps even heal them. He started out with just a few people following him, which quickly became twenty or thirty whom he would talk and be close to. This escalated to the point where in Luke 10–11 we have him sending out seventy-two disciples to various towns and cities. All of these communities in Israel were close, so word traveled fast. Francine says some came out to see him out of curiosity, others to jeer and some because they wanted to learn or be healed.

You must remember it was even worse than today. Yes, we have skeptics . . . but we have freedom of speech. Where he had full reign in India or other countries that were tolerant of other religions and philosophies, in Israel he had Roman rule and their gods as well as the Sanhedrin and the fearful and vengeful God of the Jews to deal with. Jesus now found himself in a stage of his life in which he was in conflict with both. Yes, he preached about one God, but his God is not wrathful. Jesus brought forth a loving and caring God who doesn't play favorites, for He reaches out even to sinners and loves everyone. This was blasphemy to the Sanhedrin, but the Romans didn't pay much attention to the man known as Jesus, because they were so powerful and he was not a revolutionist like his cousin John the Baptist. John had been far more judgmental and had constantly railed against Roman occupation. Jesus, on the other hand, used words of kindness to persuade people.

Jesus employed all the knowledge that he had gained in

his travels. Being a Gnostic, he was never afraid to incorporate any part of any truth or any religion that had true knowledge; he would just couch his words to fit into Jewish thought and tradition, and extensively used parables to get his points across. Being an Essene, he was influenced by not only their philosophy, but their documentation. He urged those of his followers who could write, like Thomas, Matthew and James, to set down everything they saw or heard. Jesus was not concerned about preserving his legacy so much as he was about leaving writings that his disciples could refer to when they became apostles and spread his teachings. Essenes preserved their heritage through their writings and made sure they were secure by secreting them away if it became necessary.

The reason they did this was because they were considered to be a radical sect of zealots by the Sanhedrin and Pharisees and were consequently regularly oppressed. The religious groups of the Sanhedrin and Pharisees were very powerful and influential and, tragically, as it is today in many religions, ruled their people by fear. If you were only going to help people by the pure love of God, the shining example of healing and beauty, you wouldn't be able to give people enough fear and guilt and consequently you couldn't milk them for money. Religion thus becomes big business. We see this today, sadly, with the evangelists and even with the Vatican. I'm not condemning or judging, I'm just saying this is historical truth. Look at Martin Luther, who got tired of the Church selling indulgences and split off and caused the Reformation. He felt people shouldn't pay to get into heaven.

Christ always felt throughout his life that his teachings were most important and that they must be preserved, if at all possible. His whole focus was on changing the way the Jewish people felt and believed in God. The one thing that most people completely forget is that Christ was a Jew, he was not a Christian.

He was teaching a people who had strict laws and traditions dating back to the time of Moses and beyond. Jesus always had to walk a tightrope with his teachings, because many were considered blasphemous by the conservative elements of Judaism. He had to be careful with his words and ideas, which is why he has been misinterpreted so many times over the years. We read in the Gospel of Luke about Jesus, after his time in the wilderness, going to Nazareth, his hometown, and preaching in the synagogue there, only to have his own townspeople carry him in anger to the highest hill to throw him off a cliff because they didn't like what he said (Luke 4:28–29). Can you imagine how he would have reacted? Here he was with people he had grown up with and they wanted to throw him off a cliff because of what he said. He was frightened, but he also learned a very important lesson: he had to be careful with his words.

While we are on the subject of Christ's teachings, I want to interject something here that is of a more controversial, yet personal, nature. I have always called myself a Gnostic Christian because I believe in obtaining as much knowledge as possible about God, and I have always believed that Jesus Christ was a direct report and messenger from God and love his teachings. But here is the kicker: I don't necessarily ascribe to *all* of the teachings as put forth in the Bible, and I don't feel he is the savior for all of mankind and that he died for our sins. Now, some of you might ask, "How can you call yourself a Christian, then?" I call myself Christian because I do believe in Christ's teachings and I do believe in his divinity as a special entity from God. I don't believe in the concept of a savior for mankind, simply because humankind is too diverse in their beliefs, but I do believe that God sends us divine messengers to help us who are as diverse as we are. In other words, I consider Buddha and Muhammad to be divine messengers for certain parts of the world, just as Christ was for Judaism and ultimately Christianity.

Some of you may say, "How can you say he was a messenger for Judaism? They don't believe he was their Messiah." Just because they don't believe Jesus was their Savior doesn't mean he didn't influence them with his teachings. Judaism as well as Islam both recognize Christ as a great prophet and teacher. As I said earlier, Jesus was a Jew and focused his teachings within the parameters of the Judaic faith, but many of his teachings also apply to all of us universally. The attributes of a Divine Messenger have always included teachings that are of a universal nature; teachings that can transcend culture and customs and traditions, that are just universal truths that can apply to anyone at any time. Christ was that kind of a teacher.

I have always believed in an all-loving and merciful God who forgives all of his creations in their transgressions. I have expounded on God in many of my books and don't believe God has the petty qualities of anger or vengeance, and I certainly don't believe he punishes anyone. God is perfect in his love and forgiveness. Jesus tried to point out the loving qualities of God in various ways, but the Bible says he retained the belief that God would punish the wicked and stands in judgment. Francine has told me that Jesus did not believe in those two concepts and that he never said God would punish anybody or that there would ever be a day of judgment. She insists those portions of the Bible that say he said these things were inserted and edited in by the early Christians who wrote the Bible. I believe what Francine says. I certainly differ with the concepts of a Judgment Day and God punishing anybody, and it would be pure hypocrisy if I said I didn't.

Francine says what Jesus really preached about punishment was that those who do evil deeds will be punished due to the universal law of karma, which he learned while in India and believed in. The writers of the Bible inserted that God would do the punishing and completely edited out Christ's words about the universal law of karma because it referred too much to Eastern philosophies and religions and smacked of reincarnation.

Francine also says he never mentioned a Judgment Day, because he knew there wasn't one; but instead tried to emphasize that doing good works and deeds assured one a place in heaven (the Other Side). She also says Jesus did not believe in a hell and instead taught that evil was a part of this earth and always would be until God decided otherwise; that he was not judgmental other than to point out the hypocrisies that were readily apparent to any observer; that he was also misquoted numerous times and his words were highly edited by the early Church hierarchy in the course of putting the Bible together. For example, she says that contrary to Matthew 5:17, Christ said he had come to "change the law," not to fulfill it. She said this is why he was so hated by the Sanhedrin and Pharisees. I have no problem with any particular religion, including Judaism, but I reserve the right to differ from some of their beliefs when they come in conflict with my own.

I have always been a staunch believer in religious tolerance. To say that one religion is better than another breeds hypocrisy and violence, and leads one to being too judgmental. I have always believed that an individual, no matter who they are or what their background is or what culture they come from, has the right to decide for themselves how they want to believe as far as religion is concerned. Religion to me has always been a personal and cherished support to help me live my life. To say what is right for me is right for everybody would be the ultimate slap in the face to God and would impinge on the freedom and rights of his Creations. I have never been able to understand how any person or group can say or put forth that they have all the answers and truth and that anyone who doesn't follow their beliefs is damned or doomed to hell or something even worse. They are not God and never will be, and their insistence that they are right just shows the world how insecure they are in their own beliefs.

It is human nature to want everyone to believe the way you do, because it bolsters a person's own insecurity that they might be wrong to convert others to their way of belief; but it is an illusion that can be carried away by the wind. If a person has only faith and belief that they are right and doesn't *know* they are right, then their insecurity will manifest in the form of trying to convert others to their belief. If a person *knows* they are right in their beliefs, they don't feel threatened by other beliefs. Part of the knowing is that each individual must come to their own religious beliefs in their own way. In other words, an individual must feel comfortable and good about their beliefs and also be flexible and tolerant toward those with other beliefs.

The plain and simple fact is that *all* religions have some truth, but *none* have all the truth. To build your religious knowledge and beliefs by picking out the truths of any or all of mankind's religions is the ultimate of all religions. Although it doesn't necessarily have a name or a church, temple or particular place of worship, this knowledge and truth resides inside of you every day and brings solace to your life and soul. It also allows you the freedom to acknowledge all the good in religion and do away with the bad.

You can pray or meditate anywhere and feel comfortable, whether it be in a church, synagogue, mosque, temple or whatever. You can find your haven of worship in a grove of trees, a garden, a mountain, a hill, on or by the ocean, in the desert or even in your own home or abode. You can live your life of tolerance and religious freedom in the most useful of ways, doing good works and treating others as you would like to be treated; and all the while *knowing* that whatever beliefs you may have are right for you. You can also be assured that God is smiling down on you and blessing you because you have discovered a great universal truth. It doesn't matter how you love God, for the love given to God will open the door to the constant love God gives to you and resonate in your soul.

I give my love to God every day, and I always get back the love of God. I am human and make mistakes just like everyone else. I'm not perfect and have my human faults and frailties, which I try to manifest as little as possible, but I also know God loves me and cares for me despite these shortcomings. I have been criticized, defamed, ridiculed and attacked by other human beings on my abilities and writings, but I have always tried my best to do good works for as many people as I can and appreciate those who have been kind enough to send letters or notes on how I have helped them. The people who seek my help, attend my lectures, watch my television appearances, hear my radio broadcasts and read my books are the ones who keep me going. I appreciate and love each one of you.

With that in mind, know that although I can sometimes

be controversial, I would never knowingly keep the truth hidden from you as I have researched it and know it to be. In writing about our Lord I will inevitably come to teachings that I disagree with, but I will always try to be as objective as possible and will always try to give you my reasons for disagreement. I am writing this because now we are getting into the portions of his life that may lead to some controversy. Having said that, let us go forward to explore more of the life of Jesus Christ.

CHAPTER 4

His Early Ministry and Miracles

THERE WAS A GREEK and Roman legend that said if you were truly holy or descended from the gods, you could turn water into wine. This might not be related to Christ's miracle at Cana, which we discussed in the last chapter, but I want you to understand that throughout the Bible you will find legends and myths from other cultures that are couched or hidden (like the virgin birth we already covered). These myths and legends were inserted in the Bible to give more substance to Christ's divinity and those around him so as to counter the influences of other religions. In other words, it was simply a case of "my God is better than your god." Therefore, we have virgin births, heavenly choirs, angels and miracles galore to show an uneducated populace that indeed the God of the Christians is greater than any other god.

This is not to discredit the miracles of Jesus, for he performed many. It seems he had to fulfill the prophecy that not only he knew, but wanted others to know, that he was from God. Not to malign other messiahs or messengers, but no one has had miracles attributed to them as Christ has. I'm sure that he had direct infused knowledge from God, for he always knew beforehand what was to come.

As he began his public life, he knew he would be addressing people who were largely illiterate, just as most of his disciples were. He therefore addressed people using a lot of parables that still hold great meaning and truths to this day. His parables were mainly ways to explain to the masses how to care for their fellow man and how to live life as a good person. He was much more interested in the society of the times than the politics. Even when asked about taxes he simply said, *"Render unto Caesar that which is Caesar's and render unto God that which is God's"* (Matthew 22:21; Mark 12:17; Luke 20:25). If you look a little beneath this statement, as well as many others he made in his sermons, you will see a general theme that he preached all his life. It is simply—quit being concerned about all the daily bustle of money and the worry over property and what you have here; it is truly transient and your real reward is in heaven.

It is also interesting to note that some of Christ's miracles are recorded in the Qur'an (Koran), the holy book of Islam. The Qur'an mentions Christ healing a leper (mentioned also in Matthew, Mark and Luke), the healing of Bartimaus, a man born blind (also mentioned in John), and the raising of Lazarus from the dead (mentioned by John). It also mentions a miracle performed in Christ's childhood—the bringing to life of pigeons made of clay (mentioned in the noncanonical books—the Infancy Gospel of Thomas and the Infancy Narrative of James). Both of these noncanonical books explain some of the childhood of Jesus but are not accepted by the Church as canon, or as genuine. If you ever get a chance to read them, you will understand why the Church did not accept them. For example, they say that Christ as a boy killed two boys and struck the parents of one boy blind in fits of anger (Francine says he did none of those actions).

✗ The second miracle performed by Christ, according to all of the four canonical gospels, is when Jesus cured a servant of a centurion in Capharnaum (Matthew 8:5–13; Luke 7:1–10; John 4:46–54). Both Matthew and Luke write that the person afflicted is a servant of a centurion, while John writes that the person is the son of a ruler (another inconsistency). John's is the only gospel where it is written that this was the second miracle of Jesus. It may be incorrect, as Matthew has written, that Jesus cured a leper before this incident, and Luke has written that Jesus had healed a man with a withered hand in a synagogue on the Sabbath before the above incident (more inconsistencies). We are going to find many inconsistencies in the four gospels, which cause suspicions that the gospels are not factual. They are also very tiresome, because they present different versions of the same story.

This miracle of the servant (or son?) does give us our first insight into the power that Christ commanded, however, for this healing was done from afar and Jesus was never in the presence of the person afflicted. This is also the first case of a person being healed by their faith in Jesus . . . as the centurion (ruler?) expressed his faith in Jesus and Jesus in turn healed his servant (son?).

Jesus performed many miracles while in Israel, and I will touch on most of the major ones that are chronicled in one or more of the four gospels. There are only a few that are mentioned in all four books: feeding the five thousand; converting bread and wine into his body and blood (not accepted literally by all Christians); and the resurrection from his tomb (not accepted by most Jewish Christians and Gnostics).

I'll start with the miraculous catch of fishes (Luke 5:1–11; John 21: 6). This is the miracle in which Jesus tells Simon Peter to cast his nets in a certain place and they bring up a huge cache of fish. There is a big inconsistency here, in that Luke has this miracle occurring just before he takes Simon Peter, James, John and Andrew as disciples; while John has this incident taking place after Christ's rising from his tomb! This is not a small inconsistency here, as someone is clearly wrong as to the time this miracle happened. Luke and John also describe it differently, which has most Biblical scholars thinking that they are two separate instances of the same miracle. Francine says this is true and that Luke's is more compelling, as Jesus wanted to show Simon Peter and Andrew that he had power so that they would follow him as disciples. John's account is set after Jesus escaped his tomb, and it mentions that a group of Christ's disciples gathered by the sea did not recognize him. We will get into this later, but the reason they did not recognize him was because he was in disguise. Jesus in a disguise? Wait and see.

Jesus then cures a man who is possessed by a demon in a synagogue. Before we get into this, let me make a few comments. There are numerous accounts of Christ throwing out demons in various people throughout the four gospels, as well as elsewhere in the New Testament. In ancient India, several thousand years before the birth of Christ, the whole concept of demons was invented. When people got sick they were thought to be inhabited by evil spirits or demons. This type of belief is still prevalent in Africa, South America, New Guinea, Borneo and elsewhere where primitive tribes still exist. The shaman or witch doctor will bring his or her potions and herbs and cast spells to eliminate the evil "demon" and cure the one who is sick. I have always said there are no demons and no devil and that so-called "possessions" are either schizophrenia or the overactive and suggestive mind emoting emotion in a big-time way. Under hypnosis, some people can actually manifest a blister when an ice cube is put on their arm or hand when told it is something very hot. The mind can be very powerful . . . especially in a person who is highly suggestive or mentally ill.

Francine says that these accounts of Jesus casting out demons are greatly exaggerated. She says there were several epileptics whom Christ pulled out of seizure by keeping them calm and one or two schizophrenics whom he gave herbs to that seemed to help; but that most of these "demons" were simply the Judaic belief of evil spirits causing illness of some kind, which the writers of the Bible exaggerated to be actual evil entities. Francine goes on to say that Christ did most of his healing by the laying on of hands and by prayer and meditation. He went into an altered state of consciousness to become a tube or vessel for healing energy from God. He had learned how to alter his consciousness to a deep meditative state in India, as it was one of their primary healing techniques. In any case, Francine says his healings had a dynamic impact on the uneducated masses and word of his healing abilities spread like wildfire.

Most scientists and scholars also question the veracity of exorcisms, saying there is no scientific proof whatsoever for demonic possession. Most of the evidence in this area, they say, points to psychological disturbances and mental illness. While most scientists and scholars say demonic possession does not exist, the early Church used the fears and superstitious beliefs of the masses in demonic possession to advance their dogma of a devil and hell. Many Christian churches today still have experts who handle exorcisms, especially the Catholic Church.

In Mark 1:23–28 and Luke 4:33–36 we have the story of a man in the synagogue who was supposedly possessed by an unclean spirit (Mark) or devil (Luke). He tells Jesus that he knows that Jesus is the Holy One from God. Jesus then tells the spirit or devil to go out of the man and then it leaves the man without harming him. In Mark we have the witnessing people amazed and in Luke we have them afraid, for they wonder how Jesus was able to command an evil spirit or devil to do his bidding.

We then have Jesus curing Peter's mother-in-law of a

fever (Matthew 8:14–15; Mark 1:29–31; Luke 4:38–39) and again throwing out devils or unclean spirits from many who came to him for healing. In many of these gospels at this time in his life it seems that every other paragraph has Christ doing some miracle or another. It would be consistent for the early writers or editors of these gospels to try and portray Jesus as the Messiah and to try to have him do as many miracles as possible to document his authenticity as the Jewish Savior put forth in their many prophecies. Although he was not accepted as the savior for the Judaic people, he did become, through Christianity, the Savior and Messiah of Christians worldwide.

Jesus heals a leper for the first time (Matthew 8:1–4; Mark 1:40–45; Luke 5:12–14) and tells him to not tell anyone of his healing, but to go to the priests and make offerings per the Law of Moses. This incident clearly shows that Jesus is trying to uphold Jewish tradition and law. It also shows the humbleness of Christ in his asking the healed leper not to tell anyone. Francine says that Jesus was always humble because he knew that God was the one giving him any power that he used and was always able to keep his ego in check.

Francine also says that as his fame grew it became harder for him to get any solitude to pray and commune with God. Crowds of people were not only following him everywhere he went, but as he moved from location to location he had multitudes waiting for him. Many times, she says, it was like a modern-day rock star trying to go through a crowd of his or her fans. It seems that the curiosity had worn off and now people flocked to him for healing or to listen to what he had to say. The Sanhedrin (Jewish council of elders and sages who were the judges and lawmakers of Israel), Pharisees (the most powerful political party at that time) and priests all took notice of the popularity of Christ and many in these bodies became skeptical and jealous. There were also some who sought his advice and counsel and believed in him, such as Nicodemus; but as we will see, the majority followed the lead of the high priest Caiphas.

Jesus then heals a paralytic (Matthew 9:2–8; Mark 2:3–12; Luke 5:18–25;), which carries some significance. Although the healing was great, it was what he said to the man with palsy that grabs our attention. He told the man that his sins were forgiven, which was a no-no as far as the Jews were concerned, for they believed that only God could forgive sins. Feeling the animosity starting to build at his supposed audacious statement, Jesus then told the witnesses that he had the power to forgive sins, and as proof he told the paralyzed man to arise and walk, and he did. Jesus thus showed them that he had been given the power to forgive sins by his Father in Heaven.

For those of us who believe in reincarnation, it also shows that this could have been a situation in which the paralyzed man was fulfilling karma. Jesus, knowing that the man was fulfilling a karmic obligation, forgave him the sins that caused the karma and thereby the man was able to walk. This would make perfect sense because Christ had learned and accepted the philosophy of reincarnation (which, as you will see, manifests several times later on) and knew all about karma with its cause and effect.

We see Christ's position on karma later on with the next healing, which is mentioned in John 5:2–16, in which Christ heals another man unable to walk at Bethsaida (Bethesda). This healing also has significance in that the healing was done on the Sabbath, which was another no-no as far as Jewish law was concerned. Now, this particular portion of the Book of John mentions a pond in Jerusalem called Bethsaida (having five porches), which was sort of like the water at Lourdes. As John relates the story, the sick and infirm lay around this pond because from time to time an angel of God would descend into the pond and make the water move. It was at the time that the water moved that the first one in the pond would be healed and made whole. Jesus came to this place and noticed by the pond a man unable to walk, and asked him if he wanted to be healed. The man replied that he had been there a long time, but had no one to lift him into the water before someone else went in. Jesus healed him and left and others asked the healed man who had done the healing and rebuked him, for it had been done on the Sabbath. The passage I like, though, has references to the premise of reincarnation when Jesus found the man in the temple and said to him, *"Behold thou art made whole; sin no more, lest some worse thing happen to thee."* Again, we see Jesus referring to sin as being the reason for the man's illness because of karma and that he should sin no more or his karma might become worse. Once the crowd of Jews found out that Jesus had done the healing on the Sabbath, they started persecuting him because of it; but he told them that he was the son of God and had been given the power of God to do as God would do.

Despite his fame, many of the Judaic people were becoming angry with him over the breaking of certain Judaic laws. With Christ performing healings and miracles on the Sabbath, we now can see more fully why Francine said he had come to "change the law" rather than to fulfill it. If Christ said he came to fulfill the law, he most certainly would not have consistently defied Judaic law; but if, as Francine said, he had come to "change the law," Jesus would have had no problem in breaking laws that he felt needed changing.

We now come to a miracle in which Jesus raised the son of a widow of Nain from the dead (Luke 7:11–15). The son was being taken on his death bier with his mother weeping behind him, followed by a great crowd. Jesus, taking pity on the mother because it was her only son, touched the bier and commanded the young man to arise and he sat up and started speaking. Luke 7:16 then says, *And there came a fear on them all: and they glorified God, saying: "A great prophet is risen up among us: and, God hath visited his people."*

As Christ was performing all of these miracles, he was becoming a bit frustrated, as many who saw them still did not believe him to be the Messiah. As the above passage denotes, people were seeing him as a great prophet and healer for God. It is at this time that Jesus in his frustration starts to become bolder in his telling others that he is the Son of God and the Messiah. As evidence of this we see a bit later, in Luke 7:19–23, what Christ says to two disciples of John the Baptist who ask him on behalf of John whether or not he is the Messiah. He replies to them, *"Go and relate to John what you have heard and seen: the blind see, the lame walk, the lepers are made clean, the deaf hear, the dead rise again, to the poor the gospel is preached: and blessed is he whosoever shall not be scandalized in me."* Now here again we run into inconsistency in the Bible, for John the Baptist was convinced at Christ's baptism that he was the Messiah and even proclaimed it to all who would listen. Now we have him doubting and having to ask Christ if he is the "one to come?" It doesn't make any sense, but then the Bible many times seems to contradict itself, and to many who see these contradictions and inconsistencies the literal interpretation of the Bible becomes less and less valid.

We have many more miracles performed by Jesus . . . the healing of a man's withered hand (Matthew 12:9–13; Mark 3:1–6; Luke 6:6–11) again on the Sabbath; the healing of a blind and dumb man possessed by a demon (Matthew 12:22), after which Jesus is said to be the devil by the Pharisees. But Jesus says to them, *"Every kingdom divided against itself shall be made desolate: and every city or house divided against itself shall not stand. And if Satan cast out Satan, he is divided against himself: how then shall his kingdom stand? And if I by Beelzebub cast out devils, by whom do your children cast them out? Therefore they shall be your judges. But if I by the Spirit of God cast out devils, then is the kingdom of God come upon you"* (Matthew 12:25–28).

Francine says that Jesus did not believe in an entity called the Devil and knew that these "possessions" were nothing more than mental illness or disturbance; but he had to answer the Pharisees with their own superstitious beliefs in the Devil, so he used their belief in the Devil to make his point. She also says he knew very well that the evil in the world was caused by men, which is why he was so against the Pharisees and Sanhedrin who were spouting hypocrisy. According to Francine, Jesus knew he was fighting the powers that be and that he would ultimately suffer his Passion for it, but he fought against stupid Judaic laws and their hypocrisy with every breath he took and tried to delay his fate as long as possible.

We now come to another type of miracle performed by Jesus . . . that of controlling the physical forces of nature. We first hear about this type of miracle in Matthew 8:23–27; Mark 4:36–40; and Luke 8:23–25; when Christ and his disciples are going across a sea in a boat. According to the above three gospels, while they were crossing the sea a storm came up and threatened to sink their boat; Jesus was sleeping and they wakened him and he supposedly rebuked the wind and water and the storm immediately turned calm.

We also hear about Jesus walking on the water (Matthew 14:22–33; Mark 6:45–51; John 6:17–21), when he sent his disciples ahead in a boat and told them he would join them after going to pray on a mountain by himself. Matthew elaborates on this incident and has Peter trying to walk on water to Jesus when they see him, but Peter's faith is such that he starts to sink and Jesus rescues him.

In Mark 8:22–25 Jesus heals a blind man with spittle.

According to Francine he found water that was very high in alkaline content and dipped his hands into the water and washed the man's eyes. This took away cataracts and the crusts that had formed in the man's eyes due to flies. Even today, whenever I go to Kenya, I see Maasai and other tribes, such as the Samburu, with flies crawling all over their faces, arms and hands and they never swat them away. It makes me so nervous, but I guess they feel it's useless because there are so many flies, and then the flies lay eggs in the moist tissue. But consider this, isn't it miraculous to learn that he knew exactly what would cure the problem? Some of his healing knowledge and methods came from his time in India, but he also got direct knowledge from God. He wasn't a trained physician, but his guidance from God gave him methods and healing abilities, as well as some insights into herbs and their uses. That is what all true messengers lived by . . . their knowledge, their visions and their acts.

Jesus also cured two other blind men (Matthew 9:28–30) by the laying on of hands and, according to the Bible, because of their faith. We see so many healings of Jesus described in this manner. As I have related in other books, the mind can be a powerful tool for self-healing. I have seen hypnosis work wonders on many clients, who have cured themselves of cancer and other illnesses. Meditation methods that harness the mind's capacity to visualize are being used by holistic medicine, with marvelous success against illness and disease. If the mind is convinced, it relates to the body this conviction and cures can occur. If, in this case, the men are convinced in their minds that Christ can heal them, they thereby are healed, not only by the healing abilities of Jesus but by their own belief.

In this incident we also read about Christ instructing the men to not tell anyone about the healing or that he had done it. We read about Christ saying this constantly to those he heals . . . don't tell anyone that I healed you. Human nature, of course, took over and those who were healed generally went out and told everyone they met that Jesus had healed them. I'm sure Christ did this in an effort to try and diminish his ever-growing fame, but as we read in the Bible, it was useless and his fame continued to spread far and wide.

Jesus did many more miracles during his travels through Galilee: he expelled a legion of demons out of a man in

Gadara and they entered swine, which killed themselves in the sea (Matthew 8:28–32; Mark 5:2–13; Luke 8:27–33); he raised the twelve-year-old daughter of Jairus, a ruler in the synagogue, from the dead (Matthew 9:18–25; Mark 5:22–42; Luke 8:41–56); he healed a woman with a hemorrhage problem by her just touching his garment (Matthew 9:20–22; Mark 5:25–34; Luke 8:43–48); he healed a mute who was supposedly possessed by a devil (Matthew 9:32–33); he again healed from afar the possessed daughter of a woman who had faith (Matthew 15:22–28; Mark 7:25–29); he healed a deaf-mute (Mark 7:32–37); he healed many who were dumb, blind, lame and maimed (Matthew 15:30–31); he cured a woman who had a deformity in her spine, on the Sabbath (Luke 13:10–17), and this again was a story in which Jesus justified doing his work on the Sabbath day against Jewish custom and law; he raised Lazarus from the dead (John 11:1–44); he healed a man with dropsy (edema), again on the Sabbath, in front of Pharisees (Luke 14:1–6); he healed ten lepers (Luke 17:12–19); he again healed two blind men sitting by the road (Matthew 20:30–34), and this incident is also mentioned by Mark and Luke, but in their version it is only one blind man (Mark 10:46–52;

Luke 18:35–43); and he healed the ear of a servant of the high priest that had been cut off by one of his disciples when Jesus was arrested (Luke 22:50–51). There are also several miracles that Jesus performed that I want to go into more detail on.

Jesus cured a possessed boy (Matthew 17:14–20; Mark 9:16–28; Luke 9:38–43), and when we read this story, it is very clear that this is not a case of possession but of epilepsy. The boy has a grand mal seizure right in front of Jesus, with foaming at the mouth and rigid contortion. If anyone knows or reads up on epilepsy and its many forms, many of these "possessions" in the Bible are descriptive of certain types of epilepsy. Jesus knew after he healed the boy that the boy should sleep. When I was teaching school and had an epileptic student, his doctor informed me after an episode in school that he should sleep. Now, this advice was given in the twentieth century and Christ knew this treatment almost two thousand years ago. We must remember that when the Bible was written, people were ignorant of illnesses such as epilepsy and instead called people who had these episodes "possessed by the devil or demons." The ignorance of these types of illnesses grew into a belief that is still perpetuated and believed in today and just shows how superstition can be carried over from generation to generation.

Jesus turned several loaves of bread and a few fishes into enough food to feed thousands. This actually happened twice in the Bible, once when he fed five thousand people (Matthew 14:15–21; Mark 6:36–44; Luke 9:12–17; John 6:5–13) and once when he fed four thousand people (Matthew 15:32–38; Mark 8:1–9). Francine says Jesus also healed Bartimaus, a man born blind, by taking clay and mixing it with spittle and putting it on the eyes of Bartimaus and then telling him to go wash his eyes in a nearby pool. Bartimaus does this and finds that he can now see (John 9:1–44). The Gospel of John considers this an important miracle, for it devotes a full chapter to it.

Scholars say the four gospels of the Bible were written from as early as 50–70 A.D. to as late as 120 A.D. Most scholars believe that the first book written was Mark, followed by Matthew, Luke and John. The Gospel of John is somewhat unique in comparison to the others, which is why the gospels of Matthew, Mark and Luke are called the *synoptic gospels*—for they all tell the story of Jesus basically the same. The Gospel of John also tells the life of Christ, but sometimes differs with the other gospels in the telling—especially in timelines and in bringing up other incidents in Christ's life that the others do not. Such is the case in the healing of Bartimaus, which the other gospels do not mention.

It is also interesting to note that John mentions fewer miracles than any of the other gospels, but the ones he does mention seem to be important ones. We also see that the Gospel of John is much more philosophical in nature and takes great pains to convey that philosophy. For instance, in the story of the healing of Bartimaus we read in John 9:1–3 about, again, the premise of reincarnation and karma . . . *And Jesus passing by, saw a man, who was blind from his birth: And his disciples asked him: Rabbi, who hath sinned, this man, or his parents, that he should be born blind? Jesus answered: Neither hath this man sinned, nor his parents; but that the works of God should be made manifest in him.* Here we have the disciples asking matter-of-factly if the man had sinned (in a past life) or his parents had sinned (incurred karma by having a son blind from birth) because the man had been *born* blind. Christ then replies that it is neither of these reasons . . . knowing that the man was born blind so that Jesus could heal him at an appointed time so that people would see the power of Jesus and God. This is what he meant when he said that the "works of God should be made manifest in him" . . . meaning the works of Jesus and God in the healing.

The chapter features more philosophical points when Bartimaus is brought before the Pharisees to explain how he was healed and who had done the healing. One of the main premises of reincarnation is that sometimes advanced souls choose lives that hold some dismay (blind, handicapped, Down's syndrome, etc.) in order to help others around them perfect their souls. Without these wonderful people, many would not be able to learn and progress their own souls by being in close contact with them as parents, siblings, friends, etc. The person who incarnated as Bartimaus came into life blind so that he would be a shining example to all of Christ's healing ability and God's power.

I would also like to address the miracle of the Transfiguration of Christ (Matthew 17:1–9; Mark 9:1–8; Luke 9:28–36). This incident is where Christ took several of his disciples up a mountain and then transfigured himself and was seen by the disciples talking with Elijah and Moses. The Bible tries to explain "transfigured" by describing how Christ glowed with a heavenly light and his garments turned the whitest of white. What they were trying to explain was an out-of-the-body experience (astral projection or astral travel) that Jesus was having. Christ, with his power and training in India, would have been able to do this at will and with probably more power than most, and was consequently seen by the disciples in this astral state. When a person goes into an astral state (almost all of us do this, sometimes two or three times a week; we just don't usually remember it consciously) they assume their astral body, which is the body of the soul, and many times go to the Other Side (heaven). This, of course, is what Jesus was doing, he went to the Other Side in an astral state and talked with Moses and Elijah. All of them would have seemed to be in a glorified state because they were. As I have explained in my books, on the Other Side the colors are much more vivid (see the gospel passages that describe the whitest of whites) and glowing and countenances can change because of personal preference. The miracle here is not Jesus going into an astral state, as most of us do at one time or another; but that the disciples were able to see and hear Christ, Moses and Elijah on the Other Side. The incident of the Transfiguration then ends with God taking the form of a cloud and telling the disciples to listen to Jesus.

Now, my guide says that most of Christ's miracles were real, but that many of them were exaggerated by the writers of the Bible. She says that Christ certainly had knowledge that was far ahead of and beyond his time. Lazarus is a good example. Lazarus was not dead (the Bible says he had been dead four days in his tomb before Jesus reached him), but in a deep coma. Our Lord knew this and began to talk to him to bring him back to consciousness. (Just recently, most doctors now recommend we talk to people in a coma state, for their chances of coming back to consciousness are far better than if we leave them alone). The point I'm trying to make is, again, what advanced knowledge he had; to know these medical facts that just now have come to light.

With a combination of innate knowledge, knowledge from India, Egypt and the Far East, and knowledge he obtained from his Father in heaven; along with his own psychic abilities and the power from God which he drew upon, our Lord was the most powerful man to ever perform miracles in the history of Earth. His healings and miracles are certainly a large part of the legacy he left as proof to his divinity.

CHAPTER 5

Mary Magdalene,
The Beatitudes of Christ

HERE WERE SO MANY women named Mary in Israel that even the Bible can't keep them straight, for almost one quarter of them were called Mary or a derivative of Mary. In ancient biblical times people of the same name were usually identified by adding either the name of their father or the town or area from which they came. Thus we have Mary Magdalene (Mary of Magdala) and Mary of Bethany and James the son of Zebedee and James the son of Alpheus as examples of this form of identification. I mention this because for years the Catholic Church associated Mary Magdalene as both a sinner and the one who anointed the feet of Jesus and wiped them clean with her hair, as well as the adulterer whom Christ saved, as put forth in John 8:3–11. They were completely wrong in all of these portrayals.

Most scholars now believe that Mary Magdalene was none of the women above and that indeed the above two portrayals are of two entirely different women. Mary of Bethany was the sister of Lazarus and Martha and is believed by scholars to have been the sinner who anointed Christ's head and feet with expensive oil as portrayed in Matthew 26:7–13 and Luke 7:37–49 and John 11:1–2. The Bible does not mention what kind of sinner she was, but most Christian scholars say she was a prostitute. The woman who is the adulterer in John 8:3–11 is unnamed and has no viable connection with Mary Magdalene or Mary of Bethany and is therefore an unnamed third woman.

Why would the Church associate Mary Magdalene with being a sinner and person of ill repute? Perhaps the Church knew what I know and wanted to hide the fact of the marriage and devotion between Jesus and Mary Magdalene for fear that it would take away from his divinity. The Church also didn't want women in prominence, and certainly didn't want her to be a true helper or partner or even the head disciple, as well as his wife. The early Church's efforts certainly had their effect, for although the Church has recently absolved Mary Magdalene from the ignominious edict of Pope Gregory I in 591 A.D. and considers her a saint, that edict forever put forth the image that Mary Magdalene was a prostitute and sinner, and many Christians still hold to that belief.

Let's also clear up the story about Christ releasing seven devils out of Mary Magdalene (Luke 8:2; Mark 16:9). The early Church had already decided that Mary Magdalene was a sinner and prostitute Jesus would eventually redeem. In setting up this Church-acknowledged farce, they did some elaboration of the facts with their Bible editing. What better way to confirm that Mary Magdalene was a sinner than by having seven devils within her that caused the sinning? Having Jesus release those "devils" would immediately turn her into a redemptive and saved "sinner" who would be worthy of being the first to see Christ after his supposed resurrection. Francine says that this whole premise of Mary Magdalene having seven devils is completely false. As I stated earlier, Jesus had known Mary since he was a child, loved her and eventually married her.

It's also strange that the seven devils, or demons, later on became the seven deadly sins from the Church. Jesus had learned from his studies in India the belief that all illness came from bad jinns or demons because they didn't know about germs or disease. The practice of bloodletting to bleed out the bad humors or demons came from this belief. Jesus knew he was communicating with an illiterate populace and had to use the beliefs and terminologies that they would accept. Francine says he knew the difference, but no one would have understood, so he used the only resources he had available. Can you imagine how hard it would be to tell an uneducated and superstitious populace that their long-held belief in a devil and demons causing illness was not true? It would have been impossible for him to convince them out of their beliefs and he would have been laughed at and scorned even more than he already was. He took the route of expediency and let them keep their belief he was casting out demons instead of healing illness. His mission was too important to risk being sabotaged because of archaic beliefs.

In Luke 8:3, Mary Magdalene, Joanna the wife of Chusa (Herod's steward) and a woman named Susanna and many others ministered to Christ and his disciples and were women of means or substance—meaning they were wealthy. This verifies what I said earlier about Mary Magdalene being from a wealthy family. These women and others helped support Jesus and his disciples in their travels by paying their expenses and ministering to their needs such as mending, washing and cooking. Jesus and Mary Magdalene were already married at Cana and several other disciples were also married, and we must assume that some if not all of their wives traveled with them. Jesus and his disciples therefore had the resources to travel at will and it made sense in his public life to travel with women. Even though it was frowned on to have single women traveling with men, the endless multitudes that followed Jesus made it easier because they blended into the crowd, so to speak. His core group looked like a group of people altogether in a society, and Jesus in his public life was trying to show the equality of men and women.

As the fame of Jesus spread, he gathered more and more followers and disciples. His entourage numbered in the hundreds and many would be sent before him to proclaim his arrival in places in Galilee and Judea. They would send the word to the general populace that a new teacher and prophet was coming and that he could heal and perform miracles. Wherever Jesus went, crowds and multitudes awaited him, as well as many who needed the miracle of healing. Among those multitudes were also a good number of priests and Pharisees who reported back to the Sanhedrin Christ's every action and word.

Jewish law and customs were very strict, and the slightest breach of those laws and customs would cause a person to be rebuked and punished. Jesus, having studied and gained wisdom in foreign lands, felt many of these laws and customs were stupid and foolish. He especially disagreed with the law of the Sabbath, which prevented good works and deeds from being done on the Sabbath Day. He broke that law continuously many times, according to the Bible. He forgave people their sins, which was considered to be blasphemy because only God could forgive sins, and he quickly found himself at odds with the Pharisees, priests and Sanhedrin. If he was accosted by a priest or Pharisee concerning the law, he would inevitably accuse them of hypocrisy and would give them a clear explanation of why he was right and they were wrong. The general populace were awed and marveled at his teachings and explanations, and he became even more popular.

This popularity put the Sanhedrin and Pharisees in a bind. If they tried to arrest him or denounce him publicly, they could lose their stature in the eyes of the people and perhaps even cause widespread rioting. In their jealousy and fear of losing power, the Pharisees and Sanhedrin started to plot the death of Jesus of Nazareth. They knew that they had to entrap Jesus by his own words, and their spies had reported back to them numerous times about how Jesus was constantly expounding that he was the Messiah who had been prophesied. They knew he was a threat to their power, and as the popularity of Jesus grew it also became more of a threat. They knew they could not let him run rampant throughout the country spouting his heresies and blasphemies against strict Judaic laws, but they also knew he was becoming bolder and more argumentative with his preaching and words . . . and it was in the Law that they felt they could entrap him.

Jesus was preaching and expounding on a loving God, a

God who was forgiving and kind; while the Pharisees and Sanhedrin remained loyal to the God of Moses who set down strict laws and commandments. The God of Moses was such that if you didn't believe in Him, then you would have a vengeful and wrathful God who would rain havoc upon you and you would be condemned to a life of misery in hell on the Judgment Day. But here was Jesus, sent as God's messenger to try and set the truth down once and for all. You must realize that religion at that time, as even sadly today, is based on guilt, unworthiness and fear of God.

Christ's sermons in his public life show his kindness and wisdom in bringing about "the New Law." His Beatitudes, I feel, are even more powerful than any other religious writings. His taught the simplistic commandments of *"Love your neighbor as yourself"* and *"Do unto others as you would have them do unto you."* These time-tested pearls of wisdom take in almost all the Ten Commandments except for the first couple, which are basically: "You shall have no other Gods before me and take no graven image of me"; "Thou shalt not take the name of the Lord God in vain"; and "Keep the Sabbath Day holy." The Judaic concept of God attributes to Him many human qualities like love, anger, jealousy, etc. The God of the Ten Commandments is definitely an Old Testament God that has the human traits of anger and jealousy and even says He is jealous in the Hebrew text of the first commandment.

With this in mind, the teachings of Christ were too simple for the heavy dogma of that day. This is not to cast aspersions, for people only know what they have been taught. It even exists today, for when I do my readings, people in dire straits wonder if God hates them or if they have done something to anger God or if God doesn't care about them. None of the above is true, but old norms die hard, and Christ certainly had a miserable, hard journey set upon him by his Chart for God.

Yet Christ persevered, even taking on the Sanhedrin and every type of ridicule and skepticism. As I stated earlier, he was almost thrown off a cliff and several times people wanted to stone him to death because of his teachings. Christ kept moving around, trying to reach as many people as fast as he could, because he knew his time was short. He traveled mainly in Galilee, because when he went to Judea he was persecuted more often by his enemies. He was welcomed into many of the best homes, usually by people who were more inclined to Gnostic beliefs and were believers sympathetic to his ministry.

I'm sure you can find some of the Beatitudes that he gave during his public life, but I would like to include them here in the hope that you will read them maybe with new eyes, or with a deeper meaning of his ministry. There are actually two sets of Beatitudes, the more well known ones found in Chapter 5 of Matthew and the lesser-known ones found in Chapter 6 of Luke, which many times give the same wisdom but in different words. The Beatitudes cover and address all facets of life, and we will begin with what we might call the secondary Beatitudes found in Luke.

Luke 6:17–49 says: *And coming down with them, he stood in a plain place, and the company of his disciples, and a very great multitude of people from all Judea and Jerusalem, and the sea coast both of Tyre and Sidon, who were come to hear him, and to be healed of their diseases.* (This shows how far we might say his popularity has spread, again due to the disciples going among the people to tell them to come and hear this God-like man speak and be healed of disease or unclean spirits.) *And they that were troubled with unclean spirits, were cured. And all the multitude sought to touch him, for virtue went out from him, and healed all.* (This shows that he was already known as a healer, and how can anyone miss the fact that healing energy (virtue) supplied to him by God went out from him like kinetic energy to heal all those around him. We also know that if you get rid of fear and doubt and have enough faith or belief, you can be healed.) *And he, lifting up his eyes on his disciples, said:*

Blessed are ye poor, for yours is the Kingdom of God. I feel any person reading this can see it isn't just for the poor, but it is also for those who are not so ob-sessed with worldly objects that take them away from their God center.)

Blessed are ye that hunger now: for you shall be filled. (Spiritually as well as physically.)

Blessed are ye that weep now: for you shall laugh. (All things pass and even if this life is hard, the Other Side is joy.)

Blessed shall you be when men shall hate you, and when they shall separate you, and shall reproach you, and cast out your name as evil, for the Son of man's sake. (He is talking to us, but also almost to himself, because if you work in truth with God . . . who can really hurt you?)

Be glad in that day and rejoice; for behold, your reward is great in heaven. For according to these things did their fathers to the prophets. (Again, it doesn't matter . . . you have to go with your own God and the love of God.)

But woe to you that are rich: for you have your consolation. (This doesn't mean you can't have wealth, just don't let it consume you and block your spirituality.)

Woe to you that are filled: for you shall hunger. (You never want to stop learning.) *Woe to you that now laugh: for you shall mourn and weep.* (This seems negative, but he is trying to show how fast life changes and we must know there is good and bad.)

Woe to you when men shall bless you: for according to these things did their fathers to the false prophets. (Be careful of your ego. Keep yourself in check and don't get caught up in your own feeling of your holiness.)

But I say to you that hear: Love your enemies, do

good to them that hate you. (Hate breeds hate, which is negative and can lead to evil. He also is going against the Old Testament axiom of "an eye for an eye . . .")

Bless them that curse you, and pray for them that calumniate (slander) *you.* (Do not fall into the trap of doing like for like when it is negative for negativity draws negativity.)

And to him that striketh thee on the one cheek, offer also the other. And him that taketh away from thee thy cloak, forbid not to take thy coat also. (Violence breeds violence and we also see here the passive influences of his studies in the Far East.)

Give to every one that asketh thee, and of him that taketh away thy goods, ask them not again. (To give to one who asks is divine, but be careful of what you ask for.)

And as you would that men should do to you, do you also to them in like manner. (The golden rule.)

And if you love them that love you, what thanks are to you? For sinners also love those that love them.

And if you do good to them who do good to you, what thanks are to you? For sinners also do this.

And if you lend to them of whom you hope to receive, what thanks are to you? For sinners also lend to sinners, for to receive as much.

(All of the above three axioms are saying basically the same thing: to give of yourself without thought of reward is divine, but to give of yourself with a thought of getting something in return is not.)

But love ye your enemies: do good, and lend, hoping for nothing thereby: and your reward shall be great, and you shall be the sons of the highest; for He is kind to the unthankful, and to the evil. (Do good works without thought of reward and also treat others with kindness. Also note here that again he brings out a merciful and forgiving God who still loves and treats with kindness the unthankful and the evil.)

Be therefore merciful, as your Father is merciful. (Try to be as loving, kind and merciful as God.)

Judge not, and you shall not be judged. Condemn not, and you shall not be condemned. Forgive, and you shall be forgiven. (This is my personal favorite and I really wish that more so-called "Christians" would have this branded on their soul. A true Christian would never say, "If you are not saved by the blood of Jesus Christ, you will be damned to hell," for it is not only judgmental but condemning. If you ever hear a preacher, evangelist or priest say this . . . run, for they truly do not understand the meaning of Christ's teachings.)

Give, and it shall be given to you: good measure and pressed down and shaken together and running over shall they give into your bosom. For with the same measure that you shall mete withal, it shall be measured to you again. (Simply, this means that what you give out, whether positive or negative, you will get in return.)

Can the blind lead the blind? Do they not both fall into the ditch? (Think for yourself; if you follow someone blindly and that person is blind to the truth, you become like them.)

The disciple is not above his master: but every one shall be perfect, if he be as his master. (None of us are above God, but in striving to be like God we are all perfect before God, no matter what faith or religion we practice.)

What I call the well-known Beatitudes are in Matthew, but I didn't want to neglect what was in Luke, because it shows how Christ was trying to give us a formula for life, which before that had been only esoteric knowledge. This gets down to the grassroots of life, living and dealing with everyday situations. Notice how everything leads us to finding our own spirituality. This again shows us that Jesus was more interested in how a person led their life than in how they followed the rules and laws and dogma of a religion.

We find in Matthew Chapter 5:1–12 the often quoted and more popular "classical" Beatitudes in his Sermon on the Mount:

And seeing the multitudes, he went up into a mountain, and when he was set down, his disciples came unto him. And opening his mouth, he taught them, saying:

Blessed are the poor in spirit: for theirs is the kingdom of heaven. (Poor, meaning without complexity and dogma and just simplistically loving God.)

Blessed are the meek; for they shall possess the land. (This I have always known was tongue-in-cheek. If you are too meek and mild, all you'll get is this world, so stand up for your beliefs.)

Blessed are they that mourn; for they shall be comforted. (All of us die, but we all come to the knowledge that we will all be together on the Other Side.)

Blessed are they that hunger and thirst after justice: for they shall have their fill. (If you look to be fair and righteous, no matter how long you have to wait you'll come back on top.)

Blessed are the merciful: for they shall obtain mercy. (It doesn't always happen right away, but karma works in a positive manner also.)

Blessed are the clean of heart: for they shall see God. (We all will see God on the Other Side after each of our journeys of life after life.)

Blessed are the peacemakers: for they shall be called the children of God. (There is so much dissension in this world and if you try to keep peace you are stretching your soul to greater spirituality.)

Blessed are they that suffer persecution for justice'

sake: for theirs is the kingdom of heaven. (You can almost see his passive spiritual training in India, as so many of the Beatitudes seem to be karmically driven. Always remember that no matter how much injustice you suffer in life, God always knows what the truth really is.)

Blessed are ye when they shall revile you, and persecute you, and speak all that is evil against you, untruly, for my sake: Be glad and rejoice, for your reward is very great in heaven. For so they persecuted the prophets that were before you. (I know many interpret this to mean persecution for believing in Christ; but I like to interpret it as persecution for believing in truth, which Christ was a symbol for. It also reads a lot like my life . . . with my critics and detractors; for later on Christ says not to hide your light under a bushel and to let your light shine before men. Well . . . I think I'm trying to do that, and I know after I die I will be going to the Other Side, just as all of you are.)

It boils down to right living and giving solace to all those suffering the difficulties of life and just getting out and showing your love and knowledge. Like I've always said, Love God, do good, and then shut up and go home. If you believe in and love God, then help someone else . . . a hidden light of truth and spirituality doesn't do any good for you to just sit in the house with it. Get out and help each other. This doesn't mean you have to be converting and preachy, just do good acts for others and in that way you'll be fulfilling your Chart no matter what your themes or purpose are.

Even when he taught the Lord's Prayer on the mountain . . . here we see again that he always gave honor to his Father in heaven. He never started the Lord's Prayer with "My Jesus here on earth." It's sad . . . because Christianity has made Jesus the only God and forgotten the Father and even more so the Mother.

You certainly can read these yourself in the Bible, but as I stated, read it with new eyes of love and right living and spiritual search. It's like he said, in the Gnostic tradition, "Seek and you shall find, knock and it shall be opened unto you." If you stop searching for truth, then you become complacent and you really don't realize what his life was about.

⅄ As he traveled through Galilee and the surrounding areas, he would speak about mostly the Kingdom of God and God's love and forgiveness. He was what we might call today not only a spiritual teacher, but also a motivational speaker. He was the only one who told people how to live, how to treat servants, how to forgive a son that was ungrateful, how to treat widows, and even taught them how to set up household rules, have a happy marriage and manage finances. Not unlike now, he would address and give advice on all the social problems of the day . . . bigotry, oppression, taxes and political problems. He was truly as he depicted, a shepherd leading his sheep to a pasture where they could be nourished, rather than looking at everything as hopeless.

Mary Magdalene always was with him and even took notes. When her gospel was found in Akhmim, Egypt, in 1896, it contained information that was very enlightening, and most of it was not in the four canonical gospels. It certainly indicated that Jesus shared with her all of his teachings and that she understood his teachings better than any of his disciples, because she was later known as the "Apostle to the Apostles." This would be a great honor, considering the status of women at the time. Some Gnostic texts consider her to be the first disciple or apostle because she understood his teachings so well and even interpreted some of them for Peter and James. In the Gnostic Gospel of Philip, it acknowledges the fact that Jesus often kissed Mary Magdalene on the mouth and implies that she was the most beloved of all his disciples. Philip's gospel is also one of the reasons why some scholars now think that indeed Jesus and Mary were married.

Aside from his ministry we don't ever hear about the "social Christ." My guide says he had a highly developed sense of humor and loved children . . . and often was seen playing with a type of ball and hoop in the midst of a group of excited and laughing youngsters. Francine says he loved to have what we today would call picnics, taking food and drink and going to a grove of olive trees and eating and drinking and talking about all manner of things with his disciples and friends.

He also loved visiting at not only the poorer homes, but homes of the elite for dinners. He talked with people of different races and religions, even though that part of the country was not a real melting pot. There were always merchants and caravans coming through and he loved hearing about distant lands and news from the parts of the world he had visited and studied in.

According to many artists, Christ had a very olive complexion, almost dark like many Arabs', with luxurious shoulder-length hair that fell into soft curls. Francine says he wore a close, well-trimmed beard and mustache. He had full lips, an aquiline nose, huge dark eyes with gold flecks in them, perfect eyebrows and beautiful teeth. He stood close to six feet or a little more in height (which was unusual for that day) with a fairly lean body or frame. Magdalene had red hair (which was also unusual), brown eyes and was also olive-skinned. She stood five feet six inches, which was also taller than most women of her day. I believe his height gave him a presence and commanded respect in a world where men were lucky to make it to five six or five eight and women from four feet ten to five feet. Even if you look at some of the suits of armor in museums, they are so small that you wonder who could have worn them. I've also seen the beds at some of the old missions in California, and they look like beds for children.

In all my travels, the one person I found to be tall and large in armor and clothing was King Henry VIII. I understand that Mary, Queen of Scots, was five feet eleven; but people like these two were the exception and not the rule. Most people in ancient times were much smaller in stature than people today, due to either a lack of food or poor diets—although Francine says that the Merovingian and King David lines were tall and Joseph was fairly tall, being a descendant of King David. Mary, Christ's mother, was also fairly tall for her time, so it must have been a design for notability from God, as well as her DNA.

Jesus was well built, but more on the athletic angular side rather than huge and muscular. I think the climate and all the walking lent itself to that. Francine says he wasn't a vegetarian, even though he had been at one point in India. He ate lamb, fruits, vegetables, olives, dates and fish, which he dearly loved. Remember, he was part of the disciples' fishing trips. His favorite meal was fish, fruit, lamb and wine. At that time, there were no alcoholic drinks to speak of except wine, which was plentiful and cheap. They drank wine because most of the water was bad; unless they went up into the mountains to drink spring water, good drinking water was fairly scarce because sewage from the towns ran into the water supplies. Although the Judaic people were very hygienic, they were not that knowledgeable about sanitation and sewage systems. The Romans were fairly knowledgeable about sanitation, but sewer systems of any size were confined to the larger cities and towns and not to rural areas such as Galilee. The pollution of water supplies gave rise to leprosy and all kinds of parasite and bacterial illnesses such as amoebic dysentery and giardiasis.

Jesus seemed to never, ever be sick, nor to have any type of physical malady ever. Magdalene was also privileged with good health and not to be ill or have any maladies. We must remember that the Hebrew communities were very much ahead of the world as far as hygiene was concerned. That's why they survived the plagues in Europe, and many thought the reason they did was because they were in league with the devil. The Judaic people believed in cleanliness and in not eating pork—rightly so, because at that time swine carried so much disease. We know now not to even eat half-done pork because it causes trichinosis and other diseases.

As Jesus traveled and socialized, he also, as we know, healed and taught. My guide says that only major points of major sermons were recorded, but she says he talked to huge groups and multitudes at least four days or nights a week. Sometimes his sermons would last hours and sometimes he did two a day. He usually did not preach on the Sabbath, except in the occasional synagogue, and that was probably due to his Judaic upbringing and obedience to old rabbinic laws.

Three years might not seem like a long time, but with this kind of schedule Jesus literally reached thousands of people. Francine says he spoke a beautiful sermon about marriage and children and the sanctity of the female, but it was not transcribed. We can't blame this omission on the Church, for the original scribes who had a Judaic background and archaic beliefs concerning women just chose not to write it down. I feel it's because old norms or religious teachings die hard. We have to take into consideration that even though they were disciples, they still had been raised with Judaic law that, as we read in the Old Testament, treated women as less than nothing. Old teachings put forth that women were made to work, be quiet, give birth and wait on their husbands. So a sermon about the equality of women, I feel, was purposefully not taken down and transcribed.

The disciples of Christ in more than one instance show great jealousy toward Mary Magdalene. In the Gospel of Philip, a Gnostic gospel that is not included as canon in the Bible, it says: *As for the wisdom who is called "the Barren," she is the mother of the angels. And the companion to the Savior is Mary Magdalene. But Christ loved her more than all the disciples and used to kiss her often on her mouth. The rest of the disciples were offended by it and expressed disapproval. They said to him, "Why do you love her more than all of us?" The Savior answered and said to them, "Why do I not love you like her?"* Now, to be fair, a portion of this gospel is missing just at the point where "on her mouth" is, and that translation of those three words is a scholarly "best guess" or assumption. Francine says it does say mouth and that the actual three words were *on the mouth*. Even though scholars say people exchanged kisses frequently in that day and age (Judas betraying Christ with a kiss, etc.), the jealousy part should give us pause to consider. You are only jealous of someone who is shown favoritism, as she was undoubtedly shown. Jesus confided in her, loved her, and he wanted her to carry on his church . . . not Peter, as the Bible says.

Jesus felt Peter was good, but in many ways a dolt. We must remember that Peter was a poor fisherman who had hardly any education. Most of us are acquainted with Christ's supposedly saying that Peter was a rock and that he would build his church upon it (Matthew 16:18). Francine says this is erroneous and that it was a case of the humor of Jesus manifesting itself when he actually said tongue-in-cheek, "Why would I build my philosophy on you, Peter? You have no more courage or charisma than a rock." I had always wondered (before I heard Francine's translation) why Christ would use a rock to define Peter; especially when you realize he predicted accurately, before his crucifixion, that Peter would deny him three times before the cock would crow . . . which came to pass, according to the Bible.

I don't know about you, and not to judge Peter, but I'm not sure I'd leave my teachings to someone so disloyal and even cowardly. Of course he went on to repent and teach and was later crucified upside down, but this was years later. Again, none of us can really know what we would do out of fear . . . that's not the issue. It's an issue of giving over control to someone with strength and loyalty.

This would make sense because after Christ's crucifixion, women held all the prominent places in early Gnostic Christianity. They were the ones who despised the so-called blessings and spiritual teachings of both the Judaic religion and the early Jewish Christians. Then later on we have Paul coming into the picture, and Peter aligns with Paul while James, the brother of Jesus, remains as the head of the Jewish Christians. Later still, as I stated before, the Roman emperor Constantine adopts "Pauline Christianity" and thus the Catholic Church was born with Peter as its first symbolic Pope.

I remember when I was at St. Theresa's College, in Christian marriage class we were told we were always second and subservient to our husbands and that we were to have as many children as God saw fit. I won't go into how many times I was kept after class to be reprimanded by Father Nadian, but during those talks I found out even he felt differently but under Church law had to teach the dogma. I grew to love this priest and saw the pain this dear Dominican faced in being torn by what his heart and logic told him as opposed to what he was supposed to teach. I can't wait to see him on the Other Side, and run toward him screaming that we were right and now we are free in our thoughts.

Francine says Magdalene always walked in front and to the right of Jesus and behind them walked the disciples. This could have been another reason they felt jealous. Instead of one of them, a woman takes first place next to Jesus. Of course, it would be a natural position if she was his wife.

We don't read much of Christ's mother in the Bible either. She seems, except for the birth, the wedding feast at Cana and possibly a brief mention that she was at the crucifixion . . . to just disappear. With men writing the Bible I'm convinced they just left women out as much as possible. We see in the Old Testament Deborah, Esther, Ruth and Bathsheba, but except for a few other minor villainesses such as Jezebel, the queen of Sheba, Salome and Lot's wife, who was turned into a pillar of salt because she looked back at the destruction of Sodom and Gomorrah, women are secondary players.

Francine says Magdalene was very close to Mary, as well as Mary of Bethany, Martha and Naomi, who used to travel with Jesus and his brothers and sisters. So they traveled with a fairly large core group. Mary had known Magdalene most of her life and felt like she was truly a daughter and was extremely happy to have her as a daughter-in-law. This bears up at the crucifixion when they and John (the beloved) and others (depending upon which gospel you read) stood at the cross together while the rest of the disciples went into hiding.

CHAPTER 6

The Real Passion Story
of Christ

WHETHER HE WAS CURING the sick, making the lame walk or the blind see, he was constantly preaching. He had only a few run-ins with the Sanhedrin. They tried at first to ignore him, feeling as if he was just another fanatic like John the Baptist; but as his popularity grew and the synagogues began to be empty, they became more alarmed. This came from two motives. One, they were losing money, and two, they didn't want to make the Romans angry; not only because they had their own gods, but because they wanted to separate themselves from the fact that, after all, he was a Jew and they were afraid they would be blamed for his words that went against Judaic teaching.

In all deference, let's understand that this religion had already existed and flourished for hundreds of years and gave birth to great kings and great religious beliefs for the time. Here they sat, the lawmakers and judges of the Judaic faith, with this "new" prophet, so to speak, who threatened the fiber of their established religion. The Romans at the same time became somewhat nervous, because wherever he went huge crowds gathered and this could spell insurrection.

The Jewish people, sadly, have had to bear the stigma of crucifying Christ. But we didn't live then, and if our establishment was threatened, how do we know what we would have done? Both the Jews and the Romans had a hand in his crucifixion—which, by the way, was the favorite Roman means of execution at that time. Later on, to the Romans, it became burning at the stake or a means of entertainment such as throwing criminals to wild animals; but at that time the Roman norm was crucifixion, just as the Jewish norm was stoning to death. Let's also not forget Jesus had to go through this to fulfill the prophecies that would culminate in his supposed death. It was out of this martyrdom that his teachings would live on.

Let's be logical . . . his teachings were vying against the long-standing religions of Hinduism, Buddhism, Judaism and the all-powerful Romans as well as other religions that were minor but popular. No one knew anything of this new monotheistic religious philosophy of a gentle, loving and all-forgiving God. Most Eastern religions don't have a personal God as such or they have many deities. The Judaic religion had one God, but He was unreachable, harsh, unforgiving and sometimes very frightening. So there appears on the stage of life a man who is trying to set the record straight, and he might well be ignored and forgotten unless his exit were dramatic. Let's face it, the world seems to love martyrs.

Yet here is where there is a big hole in the prophecies. The "Savior" was supposed to come and free the Jews. He was to be a king with wealth and, much like Moses, was to free them from oppression and lead them in their promised land. Christ came to show them how to be free in their souls and how to correct and live their lives so they could truly live in the "promised land" of the Kingdom of God (the Other Side). Christ did neither and yet he did both . . . does that sound confusing?

Some of the Messianic prophecies (prophecies pertaining to the Savior, and there are reputedly over three hundred) are: The Jewish Savior was to be from the lineage of David—Christ fulfilled that. The Savior was to be born of a virgin (a misinterpreted and man-made prophecy to deflect the influence of other religions)—Christ supposedly fulfilled that. The Savior was to be heralded by a messenger of God (John the Baptist)—Jesus fulfilled that. He would perform miracles—Jesus fulfilled that. He would preach good news—Jesus fulfilled that. He would enter Jerusalem as a King riding a donkey—Christ fulfilled that. He would die a humiliating and painful death—Christ supposedly fulfilled that. His hands and feet would be pierced—Jesus fulfilled that. His executioners would cast lots for his clothing—evidently fulfilled. None of his bones would be broken in his execution—Christ fulfilled that. His side would be pierced—Jesus fulfilled that. He would die with the wicked and be buried in a rich man's tomb—Christ supposedly fulfilled that. He would be born in Bethlehem—Jesus fulfilled that. He would come out of

Egypt—Christ fulfilled that. And on and on it goes. Most of these Messianic prophecies from the Old Testament are very vague in nature and can be ascribed or not ascribed to Jesus depending upon interpretation. One of the main prophecies of the Savior was to bring world peace . . . Christ did not do that.

The problem with prophecies is that they are made many times by men or women for humankind, are interpreted by humankind and are always looked upon from the perspective of living life on earth. After all, most of us only consider reality to be what we can feel, hear, taste, smell and see . . . the premise of anything else being a part of reality is purely subjective, and therein lies the problem. God and the Afterlife are for most people a belief and not a reality, and are therefore a matter of faith. For those who are more enlightened spiritually, faith becomes knowing and also a part of their reality. The problem with most religion is that it is based on faith and not reality . . . thus, although a person who is religious may *believe* that something is true, they don't really *know* if it's true. They are put in the position of having God and an Afterlife compared to what they perceive as reality, and sadly, God and the premise of an Afterlife come in a poor second. This is because very few can hear, touch or see God or an Afterlife. If we can't sense something with our five main senses, it ceases to be real to us and then becomes a matter of faith—which is a poor substitute for our perceived reality.

If God would get on a loudspeaker that covered all the world and say, "I want to introduce myself, I am God"—then most likely all of us would make God part of our reality. Or if the heavens opened and all of us on Earth saw the Other Side in all its glory in a prolonged vision, then the chances are most of us might also make that a part of our reality. It is also a distinct possibility that many of us would say that hearing God or seeing the Other Side was only our imagination working overtime or a delusion. The point is that humankind perceives reality to be the life we live on Earth and that the belief in God (or gods) and an Afterlife will always be as diverse as the numerous cultures we have here on this planet.

Prophecy is nothing more than an extension of belief and faith. We certainly don't know if something prophesied will happen until it happens, and there are many prophecies that have not happened yet and certainly many that were not fulfilled. In the case of Jesus, there are many who say he fulfilled the Messianic prophecies and many who say he didn't. Does it really matter whether or not Christ fulfilled these Messianic prophecies? Is prophecy such an exact science that millions of Judaic people are still waiting for their savior because of it or that billions of Christian, Judaic and Islamic peoples are still waiting for the Judgment Day?

It seems that if a prophecy was made by David or Isaiah or Jeremiah, it has to be true; but many of their prophecies have not come to pass. The reason I have inserted this section on prophecy and reality is that it shows how strongly the Bible was associated with people who told the future. Then, after the Bible was put together, the Christian era banned all telling of future happenings. It's acceptable to prophesy in the Old Testament, but not after the Church was established, for it did not fit into the Church's perception of reality. It's also all right to prophesy if you are a saint, but keep it under wraps and above all keep it quiet if you are not. I've often wondered how religions all of a sudden decided that prophets were no longer being born and that prophecy was pure hogwash, especially when it plays such a large part in the dogma of all the major religions.

The true story of the Passion of Christ is one of the most controversial secrets Christianity has tried to hide for almost two thousand years. Nothing that is truth can be hidden forever, because it will work its way to the top for everyone to see.

The Sanhedrin and Pharisees started to put pressure on the Roman government to arrest Jesus and bring him in for trial. The incidents that occurred on Palm Sunday, as the Church now calls it, put the Sanhedrin and Pharisees over the proverbial edge. Jesus did come into the city with great fanfare on the Sabbath, which was one week before Passover. This seemed like a blasphemy to the Judaic elders. He then incurred more of their wrath by visiting the Temple and driving out the moneylenders with a whip, citing their hypocrisy in the process. The Sanhedrin met in a special council and decided to petition Pontius Pilate to arrest Jesus and put him on trial for blasphemy and sedition. This took a few days, as even then there were many in the Sanhedrin who felt the charges unjustified.

In the interim period, Jesus told Judas Iscariot to arrange a private meeting with Pilate if possible, as he knew what was coming. Pilate agreed to the meeting mostly out of curiosity, but also because his beloved wife had had a dream about Jesus that said Jesus should not be harmed, and he respected his wife's counsel. The meeting was arranged with only Pilate, Jesus, Judas Iscariot and Joseph of Arimathaea in attendance. This meeting was several days before the erroneous story of Judas's betrayal was to take place. If you use your logic, why would Judas have to betray him with a kiss and receive thirty pieces of silver when the Romans already knew who he was and where he was? Jesus was not exactly hiding when he preached to the people in Jerusalem for all to see.

This private meeting set into motion one of the greatest plots in the history of mankind. Pilate, in meeting Jesus for the first time, was profoundly curious about this man who seemed to attract huge multitudes to just hear him speak. After questioning him about his intentions toward Rome, he was satisfied that Christ had no seditious intent and was frankly quite impressed with him, as most people who came into contact with Jesus were similarly impressed. Pilate could find no wrong in him and found him to be a gentle and charming man. Pilate, however, was also the governor of Israel and certainly knew the political climate from his many spies in the Sanhedrin and Pharisees, as well as throughout Galilee and Judea, and therein was the problem—how was he to keep order and avoid possible rioting or insurrection?

Pontius Pilate was intelligent, decisive and cunning. He had to be or he would not be governor of Israel for long and would not maintain his stature. He knew that Rome wanted peace above all else, for otherwise trade would be disrupted and Roman resources would have to be spent on downing any uprisings. He also knew the atmosphere in Israel was potentially very explosive. He knew the Sanhedrin and Pharisees wanted Christ condemned, but Pilate also knew Jesus had many followers and he was afraid there could be rioting and possible revolution on either side if Jesus was condemned or set free. Pilate was faced with a great dilemma—what to do with this man known as Jesus?

Francine says Pilate came up with an ingenious plan. Finding no wrong in Jesus, he proposed an audacious scheme that would depend upon complete secrecy, but most of all would depend on Christ's cooperation.

According to Francine, Pilate explained to Christ that he found him to be no threat, but he had to maintain peace with the ruling religious structure (Sanhedrin and Pharisees) within Israel. Pilate outlined to Jesus that they wanted him to be arrested and put on trial and that he would do all he could to get a verdict of innocence for him. If they found him guilty he would try to keep him alive, even though he would have to enact the penalty of scourging and crucifixion as per the law; but there were no guarantees that he would be able to do so. Jesus understood what Pilate was saying and knew his fate was sealed. He held out a slight hope nonetheless that this plan might succeed, even though it would involve a great deal of pain and suffering. The four of them then talked for some time on the contingencies of the plan and the role of each in it. The plan depended upon mutual trust and precise actions on the part of all involved, but at least Christ had a slight hope that he might escape his preordained mission—not without pain and suffering, but with his life. Jesus would have to be strong in not only enduring what he must endure, but also in his belief that God would be merciful and allow him to live, for as Pilate said, there were no guarantees.

This seems to put Pilate in a good light, but Francine says he was just being careful and expedient. Pilate knew he had nothing to lose in this gamble to keep the peace. If Jesus was found innocent, so be it. If Jesus was found guilty and crucified, it would appease the Sanhedrin and Phari-sees, and if he was able to keep him alive it would appease Christ's followers. No one would dare to accuse him of try-ing to keep Christ alive, and if the plot was discovered it could easily be blamed on Christ's followers. Francine says God did intervene here, however, because he sent the dream to Pilate's wife and also implanted the plan in Pi-late's mind and caused him to go through with it.

Jesus knew beforehand what his fate was to be, but this plot devised by Pilate was a surprise to him. Francine says that we must remember that despite the divinity of Jesus and despite his knowing what he would have to go through, only God knows everything and knows the outcome of events that happen. We see divine intervention even today in situations that seem to be impossible in our understand-ing, but that turn out to be what we call miracles.

With this faint hope of survival in him, Jesus, knowing all involved had to keep this plan secret, advised both Judas and Joseph to not say anything to anyone, especially his disciples. Jesus did tell Mary Magdalene of the plan because she was his wife and closest confidante. Francine says her anguish was great. She knew that once he was turned over to the Sanhedrin anything could happen, even though the Romans were the only ones in power to carry out the final sentence of execution. In a small way it's like a surgery that you know has to be done and you hope you will survive, but the agony of going through it and the aftermath is still frightening because you know anything can go wrong. Jesus didn't trust his disciples with any of this knowledge because he worried that any one of them, either out of stupidity or fear, would tell the wrong person.

Jesus also held what we refer to as the last supper because he knew that no matter how things turned out, it was likely to be the last time his disciples would be able to convene with him fully in one place. He knew if he survived he would have to leave Israel and his disciples behind or risk recapture and death. It is interesting to note that where most scholars believe he held this last supper was in the

Essene compound on Mount Sion, which insured privacy because the Essenes were a secular group.

Francine says that although Christ held a slight hope of survival in his mind, he was really mentally prepared to die. She says he felt his chances were very slim at best to survive and that what sustained him was the fact that he was doing all this for God. With this in mind, at the last supper, when he did tell them to remember everything he said and when they broke bread and drank wine to remember him, he really thought this would be the last time they would be together in life. I'm sure some of the disciples must have been puzzled over this, even though he had already told them about what he had to go through, and, as planned, he did say, "One of you will betray me." This, of course, was ordained by prophecy, and Judas had already agreed to do it as part of the secret plot. Even though the Roman soldiers knew whom they were looking for, it made the plot more believable that one of his own would point him out.

Jesus did go to the garden at Gethsemane and ask God to remove this chalice (or pain) from him. Christ was referring to his probable execution, which he knew was coming. This also proves you can't get out of your Chart. After he petitioned God, we are also pretty sure that God said no because our Lord, again invoking Christ's Chart, said, "*Thy will be done.*" Eventually, after finding the disciples with him asleep, soldiers came to arrest him, and after a brief skirmish in which a disciple cut off the ear of a servant of the high priest (which Christ immediately healed), they bound Jesus and took him away.

Jesus was taken to the high priest of the Sanhedrin by the soldiers of the Temple (it was not the Romans who arrested Jesus but the Jewish soldiers who stood guard at the Jewish Temple, sent by the Sanhedrin). The Sanhedrin priests then questioned Jesus all night, and supposedly many false witnesses were brought to testify against him. The Sanhedrin also beat Jesus during his questioning and trial. My guide says this was done out of frustration and anger and they knew they had no other punishment but to beat and flog him.

Here is where we get into inconsistency again, as the four gospels differ on a key question put forth to Jesus. In the gospels of Matthew (Matthew 26:63–64), Mark (Mark 14:61–62) and Luke (Luke 22:66–70), Christ is asked by the high priest of the Sanhedrin whether or not he is the

147

Son of God. Matthew has Christ saying, *"Thou hast said it. Nevertheless, I say to you, hereafter you shall see the Son of Man sitting at the right hand of the Power and coming upon the clouds of heaven."* Luke has Jesus answering, *"If I tell you, you will not believe me: and if I question you, you will not answer me, or let me go. But henceforth, the Son of Man will be seated at the right hand of the power of God. And they all said, 'Art thou, then, the Son of God?' He answered, 'You yourselves say that I am.' "* Mark, however, has Christ answering, *"I am. And you shall see the Son of Man sitting at the right hand of the Power and coming with the clouds of heaven."* John makes no mention at all of this question in his gospel, relating only that Jesus was asked questions concerning his disciples and teaching. This omission by John of this very important question again raises the issue of whether or not the question was even asked, especially as the question directly relates to his divinity and Jewish prophecy.

We also have inconsistency in the response to the question. Mark has Jesus answering that he is the Christ and Son of God and then, in the next sentence, referring to himself as the Son of Man. Both Matthew and Luke have

Christ saying that the Sanhedrin says he is the Son of God and then he also refers to himself as the Son of Man. This is a very important inconsistency, because it has always been a huge theological question: was Christ the Son of God or the Son of Man? If Christ was the Son of God (although all of us are sons and daughters of God) and the Christ, then he indeed would be divine and the Savior that the Jews had waited for. If Christ was the Son of Man, then his divinity would be in question and he would not necessarily be the Christ. This issue was debated hotly in the early Church, and Jewish Christians always maintained that Jesus was a great prophet and teacher but not divine, being a Son of Man. Pauline Christians took the view that he was the Son of God and thereby divine and the Savior. Early Gnostic Christians seemed to be split on the issue.

Francine says that Jesus knew he was a special entity on a mission for God and that it was preordained that he go through these tribulations. She says he also knew that all of humankind were technically sons and daughters of God, but also knew full well that he was ordained by God to be the Christ that the Jewish prophecies had foretold was coming. He also knew that the Sanhedrin would not accept this fact, so he gave them an ambiguous answer (except for Mark's rendition).

We do know that Jesus definitely said he was the Son of Man, but he also said he was the Christ. I have often wondered whether this was just a question of semantics, as the Judaic people believed that the Christ would be the Son of God, while Jesus just thought he was a special mission entity from God that was the Christ of the Judaic people. Francine says that he was indeed the Christ for the Judaic people and that his teachings were so full of truth that they eventually spread throughout the world in the form of Christianity. On the one hand you could say that Jesus had only partial success in his mission, as the Judaic people did not accept him as the Christ or their savior. On the other hand you could say his mission was an overwhelming success in that many Jews converted to Christianity and his message spread throughout the world.

The Sanhedrin then took Jesus to Pontius Pilate and they demanded that he be crucified as a judgment for blasphemy. The Sanhedrin knew that only Pilate could make a final judgment on any person accused of a crime, as the

Romans occupied Israel. Pilate made a valiant effort to try to save and free Christ and truly hoped to stop the situation right there by declaring he could not find fault with this man. He even sent him to Herod for judgment in the hope that he would be freed (Luke 23:7–12) and the issue resolved. Herod sent Jesus back to Pilate after mocking him, not wanting the responsibility.

Pilate then tried to use the tradition of freeing a prisoner at Passover to gain the freedom of Christ by having the crowd choose between Jesus and Barabbas. He was trying everything he could to live up to the promise that he had made to Jesus. Nothing worked, and the Sanhedrin-controlled crowd was now a mob shouting to crucify Jesus. Seeing the mob getting uglier, Pilate knew he would have to fall back to other planned contingencies in his effort to help Jesus survive. Knowing he could no longer free Jesus and keep him from being crucified, he only now hoped he could keep him alive. As a final gesture of frustration and self-protection, Pilate ordered a bowl of water and washed his hands in front of the crowd, saying, *"I am innocent of the blood of this just man; see to it yourselves"* (Matthew 27:24).

Matthew's is the only gospel to mention Pilate washing his hands of the matter, and Luke's is the only gospel that doesn't mention the scourging of Christ. The gospels of Matthew, Mark and John all have Pilate scourging Christ before he delivers him to the Sanhedrin for crucifixion. Luke says nothing about Jesus being scourged at all and just has him delivered by Pilate to the crowd to be crucified. Is this just an omission on Luke's part? Francine says that Pilate had Jesus whipped for the sake of appearances and also because he hoped that the beating would pacify the crowd and allow him to set Jesus free. Pilate had given orders to not scourge Jesus heavily, as Jesus had already taken some abuse from the Sanhedrin in his trial earlier, and he wanted Jesus as strong as possible to survive his ordeal of crucifixion if necessary. Pilate also was very adamant to his soldiers that this man was not to die.

The Sanhedrin-controlled crowd took Jesus and made him carry his own cross, but there were people who at intervals would help him when he fell. Even Joseph of Arimathaea helped him. This is not ever to lead you to believe that Christ's suffering was not excruciating. When they flogged him they even dumped water with heavy concentrations of salt over his wounds, which was very painful, and yet it helped staunch the bleeding.

Jesus was weak from having no food and very little water. If he had not been in good condition he would have died from the trauma of the beatings and having no sustenance. Francine says this is where his training in India helped him. He was able to put himself in an altered state of consciousness much like meditation or self-hypnosis, which helped to sustain him through his whole ordeal.

When they finally got him to Golgotha (the place of the skull), the Roman soldiers did nail Christ's wrists and feet to the cross; but they were very adept at missing the main arteries so that he wouldn't bleed out heavily. Pilate had given orders that this man was not to die, so unlike the two thieves crucified with him (to fulfill prophecy once again), Jesus had ropes tied under his armpits to give him more support. They also gave him a footrest, which the others did not have, and did not break his legs. According to the gospels of Matthew, Mark and Luke, Christ was on the cross for about three hours and it was also part of Pilates' plan to only have him on the cross for a short period of time.

Before we go any further, let's review some facts about crucifixion. Most scholars agree that crucifixions are an agonizing and slow death. Most of the deaths from crucifixion are due to suffocation from too much pressure on the diaphragm. Most people who were crucified took several days to die and eventually either suffocated, by not being able to lift themselves up to breathe because of exhaustion, or died due to trauma and a lack of water in being exposed to the elements of sun and wind. The Romans had perfected this manner of execution at that time. If they wanted a person to die a quick death, they would break their legs so they couldn't push with their legs to breathe. Victims who had their legs broken usually lasted only from six to twelve hours, as opposed to those who lasted several days without their legs being broken. Victims of crucifixion were usually hung on the cross with ropes after being scourged. A few were nailed to the cross by their wrists and usually had the heels of their feet also nailed to the cross.

One of the fortuitous circumstances surrounding the crucifixion of Jesus was that he was crucified on the day before the Sabbath, known as Preparation Day. Pilate had delayed giving Jesus over for crucifixion, so that he was crucified in midafternoon. With the Sabbath being a holy day, Jewish law forbade bodies being on the cross on the Sabbath, which started in the evening of Preparation Day, so the bodies of Jesus and the two thieves had to be down from the cross by evening. This fit in perfectly with Pilate's plan, as you will see.

Some of the gospels relate how Christ was crowned with thorns by Roman soldiers before his crucifixion. According to Francine one centurion did weave a crown of thorns and put it on Christ's head, for which he was later disciplined by Pilate. Above his head on the cross the Romans put a sign that read, JESUS, KING OF THE JEWS. You would think even if this was mocking, it would have made the Jews mad, but the Sanhedrin and Pharisees who witnessed the crucifixion mocked Jesus over it and jeered to him that if he was the Christ to save himself and get off the cross and they would believe. It was also at this time that some of the priests of the Sanhedrin started worrying over the lateness of the hour. They knew the bodies of Jesus and the two thieves had to be taken down from the cross before the Sabbath commenced or Jewish law concerning the Sabbath would be broken. They went to Pilate and asked that the legs of the victims be broken to hasten their deaths (John 19:31–33). Pilate sent soldiers to do this but also gave them orders not to break the legs of Christ because he was already dead. You will see why he gave these strange orders shortly.

While the crowd was mocking him on the cross and several priests had gone to Pilate to insist that Jesus' legs be broken, Roman soldiers were casting lots for Christ's clothing. This verifies what I said earlier about Christ being wealthy, for he had a robe that was of the finest cloth with no seams. This is not the clothing of a poor man, but a man of means who wore expensive garments. You certainly wouldn't compete with raggedy, worn clothes. It also fulfilled another prophecy concerning the Christ. Indeed, many prophecies concerning the Christ were fulfilled that day: being executed with the wicked (thieves); the casting of lots over his garments; no bones being broken during his execution; and the piercing of his body.

Pontius Pilate had what they call runners, who were either soldiers or people whom he could trust who were incognito, to report back to him and tell him the status of Jesus. As the third hour of his crucifixion approached, a runner reported to Pilate that Jesus seemed to be failing. Pilate had one of his physicians make up a concoction that would be very much like a sleeping potion, except it induced a light coma, and sent it back to the site of crucifixion. When Christ asked for water because he thirsted, a sponge was filled with this elixir and given to Jesus. In a very short period of time, Jesus fell into a light coma state and appeared for all practical purposes dead. All of this had been planned, and Christ accepted the elixir gratefully and hoped it would work. The centurion in charge had been told by Pilate to pronounce Jesus dead when he passed out and to lightly pierce his side to prove it. Because he was in a coma, Christ's body did not react to the piercing and he was pronounced dead. Joseph of Arimathaea then, according to the plan, immediately took the body of Jesus from the cross and, with Mary Magdalene and Nicodemus, placed him in linen cloth and put him in Joseph's tomb to be out of sight of prying eyes. The Jews were going to bury him, but it was prearranged with Pilate that they would use the tomb of Joseph to hide him and bring him back to consciousness. Why this is significant is because it was in a hewed-out cave of rock and had a type of stone bed and a rock that would seal the tomb. How convenient that he wasn't buried underground, where he would have died of suffocation.

Call it divine intervention or atmospheric conditions, but the sky did turn dark and torrents of rain began to fall shortly after Christ was put on the cross. I'm sure God made this happen not only to drive the few onlookers away, but to keep witnesses from seeing that Jesus was in a coma state and still breathing. When they took him to the tomb it was still just before sundown, as it was against Jewish law to bury someone at night. Pilate had sent his best physicians and they, with Mary Magdalene, worked on him to revive him and dress and treat his wounds. He rested for a time and was given food and drink. Pilate then sent word that the Sanhedrin was planning to send soldiers to guard the tomb and to move him to a safer place. They then moved Christ to recover, leaving a closed tomb and the linen he was wrapped in when he was taken down from the cross.

The four gospels relate to us what Jesus said when he was on the cross in extreme suffering and agony. Only Matthew (Matthew 27:46) and Mark (Mark 15:34) have

Jesus saying, "*My God, my God, why hast thou forsaken me?*" According to both of these gospels it is the only utterance he made from the cross except for a loud cry at his supposed death. Although the gospels of Luke and John don't mention the above saying at all, they do recount that Christ had some conversations with other people. In Luke we have Jesus speaking to his Father in heaven twice. Luke 23:34 has Christ saying, "*Father, forgive them, for they do not know what they are doing,*" and Luke 23:46 has Jesus saying, "*Father, into thy hands I commend my spirit.*" Luke 23:43 also has Jesus replying to one of the thieves who asks Jesus to remember him, "*Amen I say to thee, this day thou shalt be with me in paradise.*"

The Gospel of John also has Christ saying several things on the cross. In John 19:28 we have Christ saying in his agony, "*I thirst,*" and someone gave him wine in a sponge and fulfilled another prophecy. We also read in John 19:30 that Jesus says, "*It is consummated* [finished]" before he loses consciousness and supposedly dies. The Gospel of John also relates an interesting intercourse between Jesus and his mother, Mary, and an unknown disciple while he is on the cross. In John 19:25–27 we read, *Now there were standing by the cross of Jesus his mother and his mother's sister, Mary of Cleophas, and Mary Magdalene. When Jesus, therefore, saw his mother and the disciple standing by, whom he loved, he said to his mother, "Woman, behold thy son." Then he said to the disciple, "Behold, thy mother." And from that hour the disciple took her into his home.* Now, most Biblical scholars believe that this unknown disciple was John the Beloved, but I contend that the disciple that Christ was referring to was Mary Magdalene. To me it is the only thing that makes any sense.

First of all, the Bible relates in all the four gospels that the disciples ran away and went into hiding. Secondly, John specifically relates that only three people were there and if there was a fourth (the supposed disciple), why not name him along with Mary, Mary of Cleophas and Mary Magdalene? Thirdly, Gnostics have always believed that Mary Magdalene was his first and most beloved disciple (*. . . the disciple standing by, whom he loved . . .*). According to John he speaks to his mother and then he speaks to Mary Magdalene (his beloved disciple) and tells her . . . "Behold thy mother." Mary, being married to Jesus, was a daughter-in-law to Mary and, as I've already related, had been considered a daughter by Mary since Magdalene was a child. It makes perfect sense that he would tell Magdalene to behold her mother, and it also makes perfect sense that Magdalene would care for Mary after Christ's supposed death. It is so logically obvious that this is the correct interpretation, but Biblical scholars would then have to admit that Mary Magdalene was closer to Christ than most think and was even married to him. This would be my interpretation if I was strictly adhering to the Bible as a source, but, thank God, I have a spirit guide who has the knowledge of the Other Side to draw upon.

Francine says that when Christ said, *"Behold thy son,"* while on the cross, he was addressing his Mother in Heaven . . . the Mother God. She says he actually said, *"Mother in heaven, behold thy son!"* which was edited by the early Church to "Woman, behold thy son," to give reference to Mary instead of a Mother God deity. Jesus believed in both sides of God, the Feminine Principal as well as the male side of God or Father. Francine says Jesus was aware of this long before he went to India, where they honor both (as many religions around the world do), because the Mother God as well as the Father God spoke to Jesus as a child growing up. That's why Jesus would travel with women and made Mary Magdalene his first disciple. He, unlike the Romans and especially the Sanhedrin, tried to elevate women to a status of more equality with men. The Romans, like the Greeks, had goddesses, so this wouldn't have been blasphemous to them. You must remember that the early Church removed entire books and edited the Bible heavily to omit any references to a Mother God or feminine principal, because you can't have a patriarchal religion if you have equality with women.

You would think that the four gospels would be consistent about what Christ said on the cross; after all, this was a very important event, in that Christ was supposedly dying. It would be his supposed "deathbed" experience and the last words he would utter in life. Yet here we have the four gospels, all saying different things except for Matthew and Mark. Why? There are other inconsistencies in the portrayal of Christ's crucifixion. John's is the only gospel that mentions that Christ's mother Mary was at the crucifixion. Luke is very vague about who was there but does mention Mary Magdalene, Joanna and Mary mother of James the Less (Mary Cleophas). Mark mentions Mary

Magdalene, Mary the mother of James the Less (Mary Cleophas) and Salome (not the Salome who danced for Herod). Matthew says Mary Magdalene, Mary Cleophas and the mother of the sons of Zebedee were there. The only consistent witnesses mentioned in all four gospels are Mary Magdalene and Mary Cleophas (generally thought to be the Virgin Mary's sister-in-law or niece). Francine says that Mary Magdalene, Christ's mother Mary and Mary Cleophas were present at the crucifixion the entire time and that other women such as Joanna and Salome also came for a time.

While the three Marys tried to comfort themselves as well as Jesus, the disciples were nowhere to be found. They made up for it later, after Jesus had gone, but they certainly were not anywhere to be found while he was being crucified. Even Peter fulfilled the prophecy of Jesus by denying him three times before the cock crowed. They went to a place in Jerusalem that had an upper room where they often met and hid there, hoping no one would look for them.

Theologians have puzzled over the fact that, as spiritual and God-like as Jesus was supposed to be, he called out in his despondency and agony, "Father, why has thou forsaken me?" This is understandable because even the divinity in Jesus still resided in a human form that was suffering. Francine says one of the reasons he said it was because he had been conversing with God regularly, and then, all of a sudden, at the crucifixion God became silent. When she said that, it reminded me of Joan of Arc, who had her voices go silent at her time of crisis and execution. Evidently this was a small lapse in Christ due to his suffering and his mental state of despondency in which he really thought he was going to die. God, of course, knew he wasn't going to die at that time and evidently felt he didn't have to comment, as Christ's Chart was taking its course and had to be experienced.

CHAPTER 7

The Resurrection—
A Plan for Christ's Survival

CCORDING TO FRANCINE, one of the first things Jesus experienced upon awakening, besides an exuberant kiss and exclamation of joy from Mary Magdalene, was a profound sense of relief and unadulterated happiness that he was still alive. Relief in the sense that he knew he had fulfilled his mission and happiness in knowing that he had survived an ordeal in which he was supposed to die. Francine also says that God spoke with Jesus shortly after awakening and told him that He was well pleased with how Jesus had handled everything.

As I stated earlier, after the treatment and dressing of

his wounds by Pilate's physicians, who then left, Francine says Jesus ate and drank and rested with only Mary Magdalene and Joseph of Arimathaea in attendance. Early in the morning of the Sabbath, they got word from Pilate to find another place of hiding, as the Sanhedrin was sending soldiers to guard the tomb. Magdalene helped an unsteady Jesus dress in clothes that disguised him, while Joseph went to get a litter and several others to help. Shortly thereafter they left the tomb and rolled the sealing stone back into place and carried Jesus away to a safe place for recovery.

What most people don't realize is that the resurrection of the Messiah is supposedly foretold by Jewish prophecies in the Old Testament—namely, Psalms 15:8–11; Psalms 21:19–22; and Isaiah 53:8–11. I will quote them out of the most recognized Catholic version of the Bible—Douay-Rheims:

Psalms 15:8–11—*I set the Lord always in my sight: for he is at my right hand, that I be not moved.*

Therefore my heart hath been glad, and my tongue hath rejoiced: moreover my flesh also shall rest in hope.

Because thou wilt not leave my soul in hell; nor wilt thou give thy holy one to see corruption.

Thou hast made known to me the ways of life, thou shalt fill me with joy with thy countenance; at thy right hand are delights even to the end.

Psalms 21:19–22—They parted my garments amongst them; and upon my vesture they cast lots.

But thou, O Lord, remove not thy help to a distance from me; look towards my defense.

Deliver, O God, my soul from the sword: my only one from the hand of the dog.

Save me from the lion's mouth; and my lowness from the horns of the unicorns.

Isaiah 53:8–11—He was taken away from distress, and from judgment: who shall declare his generation? Because he is cut off out of the land of the living: for the wickedness of my people have I struck him.

And he shall give the ungodly for his burial, and the rich for his death: because he hath done no iniquity, neither was there deceit in his mouth.

And the Lord was pleased to bruise him in infirmity: if he shall lay down his life for sin, he shall see a long-lived seed, and the will of the Lord shall be prosperous in his hand.

Because his soul hath laboured, he shall see and be filled: by his knowledge shall this my just servant justify many, and he shall bear their inequities.

Now, if you have a Bible handy, you might want to read these prophecies and the wording might be a little different if you have a different version of the Bible. I expect that you will come away from that experience just as I did . . . confused because of the blatant obscurity. How anyone can figure that these are prophecies of the resurrection is beyond me. I have always put forth that there is an afterlife, a place where we go that has no evil or negativity, which I call the Other Side. Therefore, all of us are resurrected (except for Dark entities) when we die.

All four gospels mention the resurrection, and again we run into inconsistencies in their various versions. Matthew 28:2 says an angel rolled back the sealing stone of the tomb while Mark (16:4), Luke (24:2) and John (20:1) have Mary Magdalene coming to the tomb and finding the sealing stone already rolled away. There are more inconsistencies: John has only Mary Magdalene at the tomb; Luke has Mary Magdalene, Joanna, Mary the mother of James and other women at the tomb; Mark has Mary Magdalene, Mary the mother of James and Salome at the tomb; and Matthew has Mary Magdalene and the "other Mary" at the tomb. The only consistency here is that Mary Magdalene was at the tomb.

We find more inconsistency in the different versions of the resurrection, and in some ways they point more to his being alive (literally) than resurrected. Matthew has the angel rolling back the stone and sitting on it while making the guards of the tomb like "dead men." He then has the angel telling the women that Jesus is not in the tomb and to go tell Christ's disciples and that they will all see him in Galilee. Matthew then has the women seeing Jesus immediately after, before even reaching the disciples, rather than seeing him in Galilee. After they see him, Jesus tells them to go tell his disciples that he will see them in Galilee.

Mark has Mary Magdalene, Mary Cleophas (mother of James) and Salome finding the stone rolled back from the tomb and a young man in a white robe (angel?) sitting in the empty tomb. The young man tells them that Jesus is not there, has risen, and to go tell Christ's disciples that Jesus will meet them in Galilee. Mark then has Christ first appearing to Mary Magdalene, and Mary then going to the disciples and bringing word that Christ is alive. To quote Mark 16:10–11—*She went and brought word to those who had been with him, as they were mourning and weeping. And they, hearing that he was **alive** and had been seen by her, did not believe it.*

We then have Luke relate how the women (Mary Magdalene, Joanna, Mary Cleophas and others) found the stone rolled back from the tomb and how two men in "dazzling raiment" appeared and told them, "Why do you seek the **living** one among the dead?" They continue to say he is risen and not there at the tomb. The women then go tell the disciples.

John has only Mary Magdalene present and seeing the opened tomb. Mary then runs and tells Peter and another disciple (presumably John the Beloved) that the tomb has been opened and that Christ's body is gone. Peter and John check out the empty tomb and then go home. Mary Magdalene stays and sees two angels in white sitting in the tomb and they say to her, "Woman, why art thou weeping?" Mary replies, "Because they have taken away my Lord, and I do not know where they have laid him." The

Gospel of John then has Jesus appearing to Mary Magdalene, who at first doesn't recognize him because she thinks he is the gardener. Was Jesus in some sort of disguise?

Here we have the inconsistencies of which women were there; how many angels, if any, were there; whether all or only two disciples even came to the tomb; whether the stone was rolled back or already open; and whether Mary Magdalene saw Christ and when. Once again, you would think that such an important event as the resurrection would be more consistently described.

The one consistency that seems to prevail in all four gospels is the fact that the disciples were wimps. All four gospels mention that some or all of the disciples did not believe that Christ was alive and had risen. Just before Christ makes his disciples into apostles Matthew 28:17 mentions: *And when they saw him they worshipped him; but some doubted.* In Mark we have Jesus appearing to two disciples who did not believe and then, just before Jesus makes them apostles, Mark 16:14 says, *At length he appeared to the Eleven as they were at table; and he upbraided them for their lack of faith and hardness of heart, in that they had not believed those who had seen him after he had risen.*

Luke and John give longer renditions but still put forth the fact that Christ's disciples were unbelieving and frightened. Both of these gospels also relate stories that give us more insight into the fact that Jesus was alive and still kicking. In Luke we have Jesus appearing to the Eleven saying, *"Peace to you! It is I, do not be afraid"* (Luke 24:36). Luke then says that the disciples were startled and panic-stricken and thought they were seeing a spirit. Jesus then says in Luke 24:38–39, *"Why are you disturbed, and why do doubts arise in your hearts? See my hands and feet, that it is I myself. Feel me and see;* **for a spirit does not have flesh and bones, as you see I have.**" Luke then further relates in Luke 24:41–43, *But as they still disbelieved and marveled for joy, he said, "Have you anything here to eat?" And they offered him a piece of broiled fish and a honeycomb. And when he had eaten in their presence, he took what remained and gave it to them.* John also gives us the story of a doubting Thomas who states to his fellow disciples that he would not believe Christ was alive until he put his finger in his wounds. In John 20:26–29 we read, *And after eight days, his disciples were again inside, and Thomas with them. Jesus came, the* *doors being closed, and stood in their midst, and said, "Peace be to you!" Then he said to Thomas, "Bring here thy finger, and see my hands; and bring here thy hand, and put it into my side; and be not unbelieving, but believing." Thomas answered and said to him, "My Lord and my God!" Jesus said to him, "Because thou hast seen me, thou hast believed. Blessed are they who have not seen, and yet have believed."*

I don't think you have to be as exposed to ghosts as I have been to know you can't touch ghosts, and I have never had one tell me it was hungry, much less sit down and eat. Ghosts can give a wispy feeling if you touch them and can even move things or rattle around, but they are not solid to the touch. I have talked to them sometimes haltingly, but with others they are very verbal. You can see them, as I have at times, and they seem real, but then they fade. Spirit Guides can also manifest, but can't hold this form long because they are on a higher level. In fact the longer a person has been passed over, the harder it is for them to get in, because they ascend to a higher vibrational level or plane. Angels that are always with us don't speak. The only time angels speak (which is not often) is when they take human form to save your life or give you a message. But no ghost stays with you, eats with you, lectures you on what is ahead for you and gives you instructions, as our Lord did to his disciples.

You can say, but if he was the Son of God, couldn't he do all these things? Yes, but because he didn't die, that is a moot point. Again, and it bears repeating, how does this strike down his divinity? I'm sure the Muslims and Buddhists don't think less of their messengers because they didn't die as martyrs and were resurrected back to life. This does not change the truth that Christ was divine.

Francine says after Joseph of Arimathaea and Mary Magdalene removed Jesus from the tomb they took him to a safe place to recuperate and recover. It was also during this time that they put their heads together to find the best way to tell Christ's disciples about the plot, Jesus' still being alive and their future plans. After about a week of recovery, Jesus decided to go out in disguise to meet with some of his disciples, and after having a good laugh at their not recognizing him, he made himself known to them and told them to meet him with all the other disciples in Galilee in about two weeks' time. Jesus took another week of preparation and recovery and set out for Galilee to meet with his disciples.

The stories of Mary Magdalene coming to the tomb in the early hours of the day after the Sabbath (Easter Sunday) are not true, according to Francine. Francine says that Mary Magdalene never left his side, and after she had transferered him to a safe place, by Sunday Jesus was well on his road to recovery. This story had to be constructed to show there were witnesses to his rising from his presumed death, and we will see how this fits in shortly. The stone to the tomb was removed by the guards hired by the Sanhedrin to initially check whether Christ had risen or not. Finding the tomb empty, they immediately reported this fact back to the Sanhedrin. The Sanhedrin priests were put into a spiritual dilemma. Had they really killed their own Messiah? Eventually, fear and greed prevailed and they put out the story that the tomb had been robbed of Christ's body by his disciples. This is confirmed in Luke 28:11–15.

Francine says that the part of the New Testament as put forth by the gospels of Matthew, Mark, Luke and John regarding the crucifixion and resurrection of Christ was largely constructed to cover up the fact that Jesus was alive and well. Although Christ was crucified and suffered tremendous agony, none of the facts of the plot to save Jesus came out except for a few clues, which I've already touched on. The resurrection was a complete fabrication and had to be constructed to give cover to the escape of Jesus and his family—for who would search for a dead man who had risen up into heaven?

Jesus journeyed to Galilee in disguise and rested often on the way, still recovering from his ordeal on the cross. He carefully avoided any Roman soldiers, Pharisees and priests along the way and eventually went to the designated location to meet his disciples. Francine says his disciples were truly frightened when they first saw him and did think he was a spirit as put forth in Luke 24:37. Jesus did make the comment, not just to Thomas but to all of them, to touch his wounds to verify that he was still alive and also asked for food because he was hungry. All of the disciples were then convinced that he was alive and started to ask him many questions.

Jesus spent the next couple of weeks sequestered out of the public's eye and explaining to his disciples everything about the plot with Pontius Pilate and why he'd had to keep everything secret from them. Initially several of the disciples had their feelings hurt and egos bruised because Jesus had not confided in them; but after he assured them that the secrecy had been needed to lessen the chance of the plot being exposed, they soon got over having been left out. Jesus also explained to them that Judas Iscariot was not a traitor and had seemingly betrayed him at his request to make the plan for his survival more believable.

Christ went on to explain many things to them that were imperative for his escape and survival. He told his disciples that he was leaving Israel to avoid possible recapture and death. Jesus also prepared them to be apostles during this time, giving them instructions on where each of them would be traveling to preach his teachings. Jesus outlined to them how they would be going out in groups of two to help and support each other in putting forth his teachings. They were to go to Greece, Turkey, Asia and Europe. His brother James was to remain in Israel and head operations there. Before the apostles left, Jesus gave them hope and words of wisdom and love and told them all he would always be with them, whether in flesh or spirit. The apostles didn't want Jesus and his family to go, but knew they had to; the danger was too great that they would be found out and thus truly persecuted. Jesus finally bade them farewell and told them he was going to heaven, which was the Essene nickname for Qumran, until final arrangements could be made. It had been several months since the crucifixion and Jesus felt he had prepared his apostles as best he could. Francine says that the Apostles then went forth and preached to many lands and all of them put forth that Christ had died on the cross, had risen and ascended into heaven, to protect the secret that Jesus was still alive.

It was during this time that Christ had a heartwarming reunion with his mother, whom he also told of the plot for his survival and plans for escape. While he was sequestered in hiding, another great happening occurred—Mary Magdalene became pregnant. This child, you would have thought, would have heralded a big celebration from everyone in their group, and it did somewhat, but now there was the added fear of losing their child in the threat that they would all be wiped out unless they escaped. So joy was mixed with fear. Joy that the royal bloodline of the House of David and future Merovingian kings would continue, but fear that they would be discovered and everyone would be found to be conspirators and put to death.

Joseph of Arimathaea was really one of the heroes of Christ's story of escape. He was a close friend of Pilate's, due to his being a Roman minister of mines, and a secret disciple of Jesus. He was the uncle of Christ's mother Mary and was very wealthy and owned tin mines in Britain. His connections within the Roman government and friendship with Pontius Pilate were key ingredients in the plot to save Jesus. I guess in this day and age you might or should refer to this as bribery or a payoff. Money given to the right people, not excluding Pontius Pilate, made the escape for the family much easier.

Jesus then took his family to Qumran to wait for the time when Joseph of Arimathaea would come for them to help them make their escape to Israel. Joseph was busy making preparations for their escape. He had a ship built in Tyre that was big enough to carry supplies to sustain them for a long journey, thinking that in all probability they would go to Britain, where he had extensive holdings. Joseph had even arranged for a small escort of ships to protect them from the pirates who were attacking trade routes at the time. About six months after the crucifixion, Joseph came for Jesus and his family. They left Qumran and journeyed for about two weeks up through Galilee into the coastal city of Tyre. In the dark of night they boarded the fully provisioned ship Joseph had built for them and sailed off on the first tide. Jesus was accompanied by Mary Magdalene, his mother Mary, Joseph, and Philip and James—two of his disciples. Despite Joseph's suggestion that they go to Britain, Francine says they weren't sure where they would finally land, but Jesus assured them they would know it when they found it.

This, I'm certain, shows that, as always, Jesus had perfect contact with God, more than anyone else who has ever lived, including Moses, who supposedly heard God's voice in a burning bush. Even though some theologians challenge this story of Moses, I'm sure he had some infusion from God. His wandering in the desert for forty years, though, does make one wonder how strong his infusion was; whereas Jesus never deviated from his prophetic and preordained path. There is no doubt that even though he may not have always wanted to fulfill his destiny, he did it with great courage and force of will. He knew by going through his travails there was a greater chance his lessons and way of life would live on.

Here again, Jesus was in opposition at that time to some great religions of the world. Even though the Gnostics' way of life and belief system dated back thousands of years, they had had no leader until Jesus came. You can have a belief, but every religion seems to need a messiah or messenger who brings it forward to the public eye. So Christ was truly the chosen one from God who was a divinity in a human form.

Their ship went up the coast and eventually went westward and made landfall in Turkey (where, even to this present day, they insist Mary and Mary Magdalene were there) at Ephesus. While in Ephesus, Jesus told Joseph of Arimathaea to take the ship and go to Britain to establish his teachings there and to return to Ephesus in three years' time to pick him up. After settling on a date and time of rendezvous, Joseph sailed for Britain and established a Christian settlement at Glastonbury. Jesus rented a residence for his mother and left James and hired servants to watch over and care for her. He then took Mary Magdalene (who refused to be left behind) and Philip and traveled again to India and Kashmir. It was while they were on this journey that Mary gave birth to their first child, Sarah. Jesus, Mary and Philip spent almost another year and a half in India and Kashmir, teaching to any who would listen. Knowing that they had to meet Joseph and wanting to see his mother again, they made their way back to Ephesus. They spent another few weeks in Ephesus before Joseph arrived by ship. They then packed their belongings and set sail to the west. They stopped in Greece and Italy for a time and even went to Britain to Joseph's Christian settlement. They finally made their way to France, landing near Marseille. After traveling for a while in France they eventually settled in southern France in the area of Rennes-le-Château. The reason that they settled in France is vague except my guide says he was led there.

Even though they settled around Rennes-le-Château, they moved and taught throughout the area and the whole Languedoc region. We know that at least one large community of Gnostics, the Cathars, also, not by coincidence, settled there. We also know that many of the secret societies, like the Priory of Sion, the Freemasons and the Knights Templar seem to have roots either in France or England.

Why there? This is self-explanatory, especially if they were trying to protect the descendents of the royal family started by Jesus and Mary Magdalene. The Knights Templar for many years owned lands and a large castle in the region and had tremendous influence on the people. In medieval times Cathars in the area were winning droves of converts from the Catholic Church, in such numbers that the Church waged a crusade against them and wiped almost all of them out. The whole of the Languedoc region was considered to be Gnostic in nature and the Gnostics gained great footholds there because in their heyday they were protected by the Knights Templar and the nobility in the region.

Some historians have just Mary Magdalene, Sarah (whom they called the Egyptian) and Joseph of Arimathaea landing on French soil; but definitely Jesus, Philip and James were also with them. Francine says Jesus took the name of David Albengentun as a part of his new identity. Since no one in France had ever seen Jesus and certainly at this early date didn't know what had happened in Galilee, Nazareth, Bethlehem or Jerusalem, Jesus was safely starting his new life in another country. I'm not sure that many of them even knew these places existed. Remember, in those days they still believed the world was flat and if you sailed too far you fell off the Earth. Only in the late fifteenth century with Columbus, and into the sixteenth century, did explorers prove you could sail around the unknown world.

Sarah was a very young girl when they had another girl, Esther, and then two boys. Mary Magdalene also had several miscarriages. Jesus kept a low profile for the most part, but did convert many around him in the local area with his teachings, and they would become the future Gnostics, who kept his secret to their deaths. The so-called Holy Grail was Magdalene's womb that carried their offspring of royal blood or *Sang Real*, which, translated, means either sacred blood or royal blood or kingly blood. In the medieval period the Holy Grail was oftentimes called Sangreal or San Greal—meaning Holy Grail or holy dish. Depending on how you split the word Sangreal, you come up with two fascinating interpretations.

Jesus was around thirty-five or thirty-six then and Mary Magdalene was around twenty-three or twenty-four. Magdalene went out to preach Christ's teachings and many call her the first pope, not Peter. Even today in France they have the Church of the Magdalene at Rennes-le-Château, as well as in many other places throughout the world. Now, if they didn't give honor to her or think she was saintlike, they certainly wouldn't have built a church to her. Most popes didn't even get that privilege. Churches are relegated to saints, so they must have thought highly of her. Theologians in the Church had discussed her for many years, and she was vilified as early as the third century by Hippolytus as being the woman who was a sinner and harlot. Pope Gregory I in 591 also confirmed this, and she was considered by the Catholic Church to be a "repentant" sinner until 1969, when the Church decided in a very unpublicized move to admit their mistake in the Second Vatican Council (Vatican II) and declared that she was not a sinner of any kind. Magdalene was never canonized as a saint by the Church, but is considered one under what the Catholic Church calls a "sense of the faithful." Canonization was not adopted and implemented by the Catholic Church until the tenth century, so before that time saints were made by public opinion and veneration, which is called the "sense of the faithful." Mary Magdalene falls into this category, and she was especially venerated in France. Several churches were built and named for her there in medieval times.

Magdalene walked among the people and did many good works and constantly preached the teachings of Jesus. Christ kept more in the background and devoted himself to his writings, some of which were attributed to Philip. Philip and James, using their own names, wrote down as scribes the direct words of Jesus constantly, keeping an accurate record of any sermons and teachings that he gave to the people. Francine says that Jesus also helped James and Magdalene in writing their gospels.

The gospels of Philip and James were found at Nag Hammadi in Egypt in 1945, but the Gospel of Mary Magdalene was acquired in 1896 in Akhmim, Egypt, by Germans and was called the Berlin Codex. Mary's gospel is not part of the Nag Hammadi library as many believe, but was not really translated until the 1950s. None of these discovered gospels are originals, but they certainly hadn't been tampered with like the Old and New Testament writings, which have been copied and edited thousands of times.

You can lose the true meaning in one translation, let alone in thousands copied by hand, especially when it's from Aramaic into Greek or Latin, etc.

There are even some words that become completely misinterpreted, such as sin. The word *sin* was originally an archery term that meant "missing the mark." So you just take out another arrow and bow and try again. The Hebrew word *Sheol* was interpreted to mean hell or Hades, but in actuality was the name of a constantly burning dump outside Jerusalem. So put it all together and then add a demon or a so-called mythological fallen angel called Lucifer and you have enough to scare an uneducated populace into giving money for fear of damnation, which leads to control. If you don't believe the way the Church does, then you're damned. Yet God is supposed to be all-loving, all-knowing, all-forgiving and omnipotent. How could He condemn those the Church sentenced to everlasting damnation? This earth is the place of negativity, dissension and evil; but it's really a temporal plane for learning or a school for the soul. If there is no negativity and evil, how do we know what is good? How would we know what our souls are made of and what we can endure that tests our mettle and makes our souls learn and expand in spirituality?

My research has naturally come through infusion from God (all things do), my life's experience and doing twenty readings a day for over fifty years. But in living life on this earth plane all of us have the opportunity to learn; and like a part of my favorite prayer, "My soul does magnify the Lord," we all have the opportunity to glorify the Lord with our actions.

Those who became aware of the secret truth of Christ's life—whether it was the Knights Templar later on in time or the people in the villages of France who lived with Jesus—ferociously guarded the secret and were very protective of Jesus and his family. The people around Jesus and his family in France became a new type of Gnostic, discarding the old theories of Gnosticism that prevailed up to that time and embracing the real teachings of Jesus . . . not the teachings in the New Testament that had been highly edited by the early Church. These people became the first real Gnostic Christians, not concerned with the question of divinity, but with the wonderful and beautiful teachings that Jesus gave them. Truth is truth and the question of divinity has very little to do with it.

Christ's mother, Mary, died about ten years after their arrival in France. Jesus was with her to the end, as were the children and Magdalene. Joseph of Arimathaea died four years later, so it was then just James, Philip, Magdalene, Jesus and the four children. Jesus would hold small sermons, with the children of the villages in the area sitting around him, and they became the future Gnostics who put forth his teachings. He would also give sermons for any who would listen, but those were fairly infrequent. Francine says that Jesus loved children and knew that they were the future and would carry his teachings for generations. Jesus also did a few healings from time to time, but was careful to be low-key about his healing abilities.

Magdalene, on the other hand, was very proactive in the community, teaching women to give spiritual advice and even what we might call the sacraments. They performed baptisms, counseled and even performed marriages. They also studied other religions, theologies and even philosophies that were available, in a type of study group, with open discussions on the merits or fallacies of each.

Women were the first priests; even historians agree on this fact. Strangely enough, women were also becoming spiritual teachers in other parts of the world, which also led later on to the Holy Inquisition. This secured once and for all that all women should keep their place or be branded as witches or heretics. France does play another part in the Joan of Arc saga, which is a book in itself. There was a lot of spirituality that came out of France, due in no small way to the teachings of Jesus and Mary Magdalene.

After spending more than forty years in France, Jesus died at around the age of eighty-six, which was very old for that time. Magdalene lived twenty years beyond him, into her nineties. Magdalene was venerated by the local populace almost as a saint or pope would be later on. She healed, did good works, taught and gave sermons. One of their sons went to Greece and the other went to Rome, but Sarah and Esther stayed in France. With Magdalene's help, they set up small and sometimes large conclaves of Gnostics that spread to Spain, Portugal, the British Isles and even to the Far Eastern countries such as India. These Gnostics didn't take hold in India and the Far East as they did in Europe, perhaps because they had been so steeped in their own religions of Hinduism, Buddhism, etc. Despite their failure there, they were not persecuted in any way, as there is perhaps nowhere on this earth where religions reside side by side with as much tolerance as they do in India. Oh, there have been some insurrections and persecution, for man will be man, but nothing like the seemingly endless conflict between the people of Israel and the Palestinians. In India you will see temples, mosques and churches sitting right next to each other.

When Jesus and Magdalene left this plane, they were aware of their Charts and knew that it would be years before their true story would be told. Above all, their lives were dedicated to the true God without dogma or fear. But theirs is probably one of the greatest love stories of all time, surpassing Hèloïse and Abelard or Romeo and Juliet. They were totally dedicated to each other and of one mind in loving God and bringing forth truth.

Those who knew the truth were fiercely protective of it, and from that protection secret societies eventually evolved because of the persecution of the Church. The Church, which really wanted supreme patriarchal power, was out of control because no one person or group was strong enough to stop it. It already ruled kings and the nobility, had vast amounts of land and holdings and was extremely wealthy. Corruption was running rampant and the Church was clearly abusing its power with the overthrow of kings, and persecuting Gnostics and other sects and religions with crusades and the Inquisition. Holy wars and torture and death became its tools . . . all in the name of God. So secret societies were formed and went underground to protect the lineage of the Holy Bloodline and to preserve freedom of worship beyond the reach of the Church. True, some of them became corrupt with power in their own right, but that still didn't affect what they knew; they just used that power wrongly.

Christ's life was basically peaceful and happy after he went to France, and he was farseeing enough to know that no matter how long it took, the truth would eventually come out. He did know it would be in our time, not his, that it would be many hundreds of years. He also knew that when this truth was revealed there would be controversy because of the power of the Church and all the lies and deceptions; but in the final analysis it would be like anything else—that those who believe will, and those who don't, won't.

Those of us who believe in the divinity of Christ and follow his words and teachings know that his suffering and even his necessary self-imposed exile were not in vain; that what he was against was existing religions that were so dogmatic in nature that they completely missed the true nature of God. He probably didn't realize that his teachings would be corrupted by men who would build a powerful, wealthy and huge religion that would control with dogma and fear. Jesus didn't go to church or temple and tried to teach everyone to seek and find the truth in their own temple without hate, remorse or fear. He brought us the true God, but those after him formed an organization that decided that money, power and politics were more important, and they became even more rabid in seeking these things.

It seems the pendulum has to swing wildly before it finally centers itself. I am by no means trying to put myself above anyone else. God knows I've written enough about my life and blunders, but I have to say that, in writing this book, I felt our Lord with me every step of the way. It was as if, should I hesitate about what I knew, Jesus would say, "Don't be afraid, the truth will come out."

We Gnostics are Christians through and through, and if I or any of the others who believe this way had come out with this at any other time but now, we would have probably been burned at the stake or tortured. I try, as all Gnostics now and down through the eons of time have done, to live a good life, love God and then go home.

CHAPTER 8

The True Apocalypse

RELIGION FOR MANY is a great source of solace and a chance to worship their perceived God or Divinities as they choose. There are certainly many truths in all religions, but there are also obvious fallacies that are based on mythology, dogma and tradition. Since time primordial humankind has always found the need to worship some being or power that is greater than himself/herself; whether it was the ancient caveman who worshipped the sun or perhaps a strong beast or even some aspect of nature, or the pomp of some religious practice or ceremony. One of the first things that were noticed by humankind was the duality that existed in creation . . . from the duality of the male and female in nature to the duality of behavior, which was classified as good and evil. It is the latter that we will concentrate on, as it has its greatest impact in the formulation of the religions of mankind.

From time immemorial on this earth humankind has always recognized power in its many guises, whether it was the chief of the tribe, king or queen, religious leader, political leader or even Mother Nature. Ancient man looked at natural disasters as omens or the wrath of some god or another—why else would an earthquake or volcano or flood destroy their homes? Today we look at those beliefs and most of us realize that they were not caused by any god but by the forces of nature that from time to time create a disaster. Our scientists tell us that certain climatic or atmospheric conditions cause storms, which in turn can intensify into hurricanes, cyclones, floods, etc. We accept this, acknowledge the wisdom of science and now hold a healthy respect for Mother Nature rather than giving sacrifice to a wind god, a fire god or a god who is venting his wrath. Times change, and education and discoveries in science have given us a different perspective . . . or have they?

New scientific discoveries and more education change our way of thinking and outlook on life almost every day. We progress from antiquated beliefs such as that the world is flat to the common knowledge that the Earth is an insignificant planetary sphere in what appears to be an unendingly large universe made up of trillions of planets and suns that have incomprehensible distances between them (whew!). New discoveries in medicine have changed our outlook on illness and disease. No longer can we say, as ancient man did, that illness or disease is caused by the gods taking out their vengeance or that evil demons have inhabited the body. Science and technology have opened up new worlds of knowledge to us, and one could say that is both good and bad. We have marvelous instruments of technology that help us in our daily living, medical treatment and medicines that have extended our lives and eased our suffering; but we also have weapons of mass destruction that can annihilate millions in the blink of an eye. New advancements in civilization bring many good things, but they also create new problems for us all to solve. This doesn't mean that change is bad, but we have to adapt to change and its potential problems more quickly than ever before.

Conversely, if we refuse to change certain problem areas in our planetwide society, those problems may lead to more dissension, more wars and bloodshed and more human suffering. Problems such as racial, ethnic or religious bigotry; famine and disease; fighting over land and natural resources; population control; and environmental issues are not going away and must be fixed. How do we solve these still existing problems derived from the nature of man? Certainly neither one individual nor even one nation is going to solve these woes, because you are dealing with inherent emotions and beliefs such as: greed, vengeance, judgment, ethnic and religious beliefs, apathy, nationalism (both political and religious), the quest for power, hypocrisy and a general lack of spirituality. On the surface it would appear to be almost hopeless that even one of these problems will be solved, let alone all of them. Nations and groups and individuals have been trying for years to solve them, with very little success. One of the cornerstones of society that could fix or lessen these problems is religion. But therein lies a problem.

There is no area of human endeavor that is more diversified than the religions of humankind. They are also archaic, steeped in traditions and dogmas and—perhaps worst of all—refuse to change or are very slow to change. I guess you might say that all of the major religions put forth the concept that their founders knew best and still basically adhere to their fundamental beliefs whose origins range from about fifteen hundred years to over four thousand years ago. Very few, if any, have made any radical changes to their dogma or beliefs, even though many have been found to be archaic and meant for people in ancient times. Steeped in stubbornness and tradition, most religions refuse to change in a world that needs new infusion from religion on modern-day problems. A prime example of this lack of change is the apocalyptic writings that still reside in most religions today.

Let's first explore the meaning of the word apocalypse. Most people think that it means "the end of the world," but in actuality it means to reveal or disclose to certain privileged people (messengers or messiahs) information either about God or the future that is hidden from the mass of humankind. Although Judeo-Christian-Islamic tradition interprets the Apocalypse to be the end of the world as we know it, there are significant reasons why they do so.

Beliefs such as the resurrection of the dead, judgment day, heaven and hell, are all made explicit in the apocalyptic literature of all of these religions and are an integral part of their philosophies to "control the masses with fear."

Think about it: religions use these apocalyptic writings to promote the premise of Satan or the Devil, a place of eternal suffering which is called hell, and the real kicker, that everyone's soul will be judged and will either go to hell or go to heaven for eternity. Of course, if you follow your religion faithfully and do what the clerics tell you to do, you just might be able to go to heaven if you give them enough money, adhere to their faith and dogma and certainly don't explore or educate yourself to reveal their hypocrisy and untruths to free yourself from being controlled by fear.

The Eastern religions of Hinduism and Buddhism are not harsh and fear-based like the Judeo-Christian-Islamic religions in their apocalyptic literature. Hinduism and Buddhism (a literal offshoot of Hinduism) believe in what they call "Pralay," which is the ending of the world by natural means such as disasters caused by Mother Nature. With all the environmental problems we have, such as global warming and a progressing polar tilt, this seems to me to hold the most probability for an ending of the world, if indeed that comes to pass. Christ said several times that no man can predict the end of times and I agree with this statement, as ultimately God is the one to determine our fate.

With that in mind, let's examine the New Testament Book of the Revelation or the Apocalypse (depending upon which version of the Bible it is in). This book is also referred to as the Revelation of Saint John the Divine, the Apocalypse of John, or the Book of Revelation of Jesus Christ, the Messiah. This book is very controversial because not only is it a book based on fear, but there is constant debate as to whether or not it is absolute truth.

The truth is that none of it applies to today's world any more than it did during the time it was written or the time of the Black Plague, or World War I or II. There isn't any truth in the so-called Rapture, unless you want to look at it as people coming to the truth about love, peace, no bigotry or judgment or war. In fact, the so-called Rapture is not even in the Book of Revelation and is only mentioned in Thessalonians I (4:13–17), which is purported to be a letter from Saint Paul, the self-proclaimed disciple (Pauline Christianity again). Do not let yourself be drawn into any group that paralyzes you with fear or envelops you into any insane cult or church that refers to the Rapture and being one of the "chosen ones" who will ascend into heaven with Christ. Realize again that God does not have human qualities to play favorites. We are all His/Her children and life is pain and learning enough.

Once in a while I will get a person at my door handing out literature on the Jehovah's Witnesses (who believe in the Rapture and that only a certain number of souls will be saved). At one time they actually gave out the number of souls that would be saved and I always used to ask them, "Which number are you?" with tongue in cheek. Since that time, they changed it to an "undetermined" number of souls. I certainly don't mean to disparage any church or belief, but sometimes conservative churches or religions make themselves look foolish.

Another belief that many hold is that the Antichrist is in the Book of Revelation. The truth is that the Antichrist is not mentioned in Revelation and is only mentioned in two places in the Bible: John I (2:18–22) and John II (1:7).

The problem here is that many Christian scholars have inserted through interpretation the presence of the Antichrist, but the Book of Revelation, again, does not actually mention him.

Every century has predicted the end of days. I myself feel we are not at the end of the world, just the end of this schematic of people coming in to perfect themselves. I know the world will survive, but I'm sure much of humankind won't. We are in a warming trend and a progressive polar tilt. We have destroyed our atmosphere with smoke, pollution, etc., but the world will have its revenge on us. What I also base this on is that about 90 percent of people are on their last life. Never in over fifty years of doing readings, has it been that high. Why? Because this part of our learning process is over. I'm sure we go on learning on the Other Side or on other planets, but, again, I do believe what our Lord said, that no man can predict the end of times or no one can predict the end of the world. The world is one thing; human life is another.

The "John" who was the writer of the Book of Revelation is generally believed by most scholars to have been the apostle John the Beloved (John the Divine), but in actuality no one really knows who the writer of this book was. This is the case with all the canonical gospels and is also the reality here. What we do know is that it was a dream, or at least was purported to be a dream, and there was a reason for this. Many people in that time put much faith in dreams and if they didn't the author could fall back on the excuse that "it was only a dream." Either way, this "John" was hedging his bets that he wouldn't get any repercussions. It is much like Nostradamus writing in couplets that were cleverly designed so he wouldn't be persecuted in the time of the Inquisition.

Many historians, and even some theologians, feel this was nothing more than an anthology or symbolic writing of what was going on politically at the time. It is likened to other books like *Gulliver's Travels*, which was a treatment of the political climate at the time of its writing. Many believe, and Francine confirms this, that Revelation was written during the bloody period of Nero's reign, which would put it in the period 64–68 A.D. (C.E.). The early Church hotly debated whether or not it should include the book of Revelation in the Bible. It was put in just before the Bible was canonized and redone by the Church about

350 A.D. The early Church leaders felt it put the frosting of fear on the cake, so to speak, and gave them writing to back up their dogmas of the resurrection of the dead, judgment, hell, heaven and Satan.

If someone today was afraid of reprisal and were to write about Bush, Clinton, Nixon, etc., or whoever they felt was corrupt, unfair and given to greed and temptation, they would write a symbolic treatment in the form of a metaphorical essay or book. Whether it's the monster that rises from the sea (the leader or Nero, Roman in this case) or the seven seals (like the seven plagues in the time of Moses or the Seven Hills of Rome), the symbolism is readily apparent. If indeed the writing was apocalyptic and not a symbolic analogy on the Romans, the world should have ended at that time.

The Book of Revelation seems to take precedence over so many of the books of the Bible. Remember, again, the author is unknown (as most all the writers of the Bible are), but Francine says he was a citizen of Rome who had a dream about what was going on in the political and religious climate of the day, around 64 A.D.

The first, second and third chapters of Revelation are

instructions and admonitions—supposedly they were written to seven bishops in Asia who presided over seven churches. The following chapters are prophecies of things to come, particularly about the end of the world. The book of Revelation supposedly was written in Greek on the island of Patmos, where this "John" was supposedly banished by the Roman emperor. He starts out by bemoaning the fact of his banishment, but says that his words come directly from God in the form of this revelation from Jesus Christ.

In the letters to the bishops of the seven churches, the writer rails against the sins of mankind and also seems to admonish the churches. In chapter 2:9, in his letter to the church at Smyrna, it says: "*I know thy tribulation and thy poverty, but thou art rich; and that thou art slandered by those who say they are Jews and are not, but are a synagogue of Satan.*" In his letter to the church of Pergamum he writes in 2:13, "*I know where thou dwellest, where the throne of Satan is; and thou holdest fast my name and didst not disown my faith, even in the days of Antipas, my faithful witness, who was slain among you where Satan dwells.*" He goes on to reprimand each of the seven churches, saying for example in

2:20–21 to the church at Thyatira, *"But I have against thee that thou sufferest the woman Jezebel, who calls herself a prophetess, to teach, and to seduce my servants, to commit fornication, and to eat of things sacrificed to idols. And I gave her time that she might repent, and she does not want to repent of her immorality."* Each church is given a reprimand and it gives one the feeling that he is referring to the churches as if they are a potential Sodom and Gomorrah (cities that God supposedly destroyed because they lived in sin). After he rails against the churches and what he feels is wrong with the religion of the day, he launches into a not very well disguised tirade against politics by using symbology. It was one thing to spout religious principles, but against politics you were courting death. Remember, this whole book is supposedly Jesus relating all of these words to the unknown author John. This reveals a slight inconsistency, for as we read in the gospels, Christ is not interested in politics.

The book of Revelation goes on, with this unknown John being taken up into heaven and seeing God on his throne with twenty-four elders about with crowns on their heads and also four living creatures—a lion, calf, eagle and some type of creature with the face of a man. You can already see how bizarre this tale is, for the creatures have eyes before and behind and each has six wings. We then read about the author seeing a scroll at the right hand of God with seven seals. No one can open the scroll except Jesus, and the author sees him as a lamb. The book then relates how Jesus breaks the seals and lets loose the four horsemen of the Apocalypse, among other things. We then have seven angels with trumpets, which they sound, and destruction rains upon the earth. We then have the author John eat the scroll that had seven seals, and he supposedly is then a prophet.

We then have various beasts come into play that are supposed to be manifestations of Satan, and John gives his number as 666. The mark of the beast was really referring to Nero, whose address was 666, and some historians say it was also his name in Hebrew (which has number values for letters). Regardless, many feel that this refers to the Roman emperor Nero and many look on him as the Antichrist. The Antichrist has been thought to be everything from a secret society to the Church to bar code technology. Many think that all technology is the prelude to the Antichrist.

In early times of the Roman Empire, no one could buy or sell unless they were from the house of Caesar. Again we see symbolism overriding the underlying true political story line of what was going on. The beast is the social regime that eats people alive, just as we could create a beast to represent our taxes that we feel are eating us alive.

The book continues to describe various hideous beasts representing the power of Satan and how mankind is destroyed with plagues. Then we have Jesus coming down to do battle with Satan and Satan is defeated and chained up for a thousand years. John then gets into the Judgment Day, where God supposedly judges all men.

When will Christ come and save the believers and strike down the unbelievers? This question has been asked for centuries, and there have been many who have predicted the answer. So far, no one knows and no one has been right. The Judaic people have waited for their Messiah since their very beginnings, and Israel has been attacked and conquered numerous times. When Israel was granted its independence in 1948, to many this event started the countdown of the battle between Christ and the Antichrist. Some people point to earthquakes and natural disasters and say the end is coming. Some felt that 1988 would be the end, and some say 2012 is the end because the Mayan calendar ends then.

William Miller, a poorly educated farmer who became a self-proclaimed preacher, revived the apocalyptic movement in 1831 by predicting the end of the world by March 22, 1844. He became very popular and had a following in the thousands. When March 22 came around there was no end of the world, but a follower said that William had forgotten to add the time for the switch from B.C. to A.D. and they recalculated the new time for the end of the world to be October 22, 1844. Again the time came and went and to thousands of followers it was called "the Great Disappointment." Many of Miller's followers eventually became Jehovah's Witnesses or Seventh Day Adventists.

We still have strong apocalyptic beliefs in conservative and evangelical churches today that use the Book of Revelation as a tool. It seems that every time you hear an evangelist, they say the end of world is near. The good will be rewarded when Christ comes and the bad (sinners) will be cast down to everlasting hell (they seem to conveniently forget that Christ said no one could predict the end of days). The ones left behind will be those who didn't accept Christ (then what about all the good people who aren't Christian?). The Judaic people will be persecuted, the world will experience famine and earthquakes and one third of the world's population will die. (This sounds like the Holocaust all over again, and this is not only judgmental but bigoted and again puts forth a God who is partial to certain groups of people). Apocalyptic preachers say that Satan will come to wipe out the earth and then Christ will come and vanquish Satan and take up to heaven all the believers. This type of message is almost like one that could be attributed to the supposed Antichrist, because it is full of bigotry and judgment and allows only Christians to be saved.

The Book of Revelation also supports the Christian concept of hell and a Judgment Day, which is exactly why the early Church wanted it included in the Bible. Hell wasn't even a consideration or even discussed until the Book of Daniel in the Old Testament, which is also one of the most powerful apocalyptic writings of Judaism. This was because most scholars, and again some liberal theologians, felt that people were straying from the Judaic religion or Judaic Law.

What better way to keep people in tow than to give them a concept of eternal torture or damnation? Even St. Augustine in his *City of God* condemns practically all sexual activity because it will surely send you to hell. This is amazing, because for years Augustine committed every crime against these rules. So much so that history tells us his mother prayed for thirty years that his soul would be saved. It's interesting also to note that he wrote this when he was very old and probably all feelings of sexuality were used up or he wasn't capable of indulging his vices.

All the major religions have a concept of heaven and hell, but each differs from the others in one or more ways. The Judaic term for hell is Sheol, but it is more of a dark place where the body and soul reside, almost as in a holding place until the world ends and the Judgment Day commences. At the time of judgment good souls will go to heaven. In the religion of Islam, Jahannam is their term for hell and Jannah is their term for paradise or heaven. The Judgment Day is referred to as Qiyamah, which Allah can enact at any time. Muslims believe that souls that go to Jahannam (hell) reside there only for a certain time, depending upon the gravity of their bad deeds. They also believe in a savior called the Mahdi, who will come and, with Jesus Christ, help to defeat the ad-Basjal (their term for a type of Antichrist). The Hindu term for hell is Naraka, but it is more a state of demotion for the soul. The soul becomes lower in spirituality and advancement if bad deeds are done and then karma will be enacted and they will live their next life in a lower class or form. The Hindu word for heaven is Swarga, which, again, is a state of advancement for the soul and the soul no longer has to reincarnate.

Then we have Dante's Inferno in *The Divine Comedy* coming along that gives us the nine degrees of hell. This book was widely read and used by the Church to be an adjunct to the Bible. Missionaries historically would use the fear of hell to convert people of other lands or those who had strayed. Hell became a much more powerful tool than heaven or God or Christ, for it converted the uneducated masses with a promise of eternal damnation if they didn't join the Church.

The Church, becoming alarmed that this was too harsh, decided to implement Purgatory. This gave people a stepping-stone to wait upon, rather than having no other option than to go directly to hell. The Church also created

Limbo for unbaptized babies or people who were not sanctified by being baptized. Nowhere in the Bible do you read about Purgatory or Limbo, and neither the early Bible, nor even the Judaic scrolls, ever mention hell.

Now, with that in mind, we get back to this unknown John who has a dream, and because it fit into the fear theme of what the early Church and its popes put forth, they place it into the Bible; not realizing that someday the people would become more literate in the world and figure out that the Book of Revelation was a symbolic treatment of the politics of the day. Many educated people who read it come away with the very real thought that this author John was absolutely insane and surely needed help.

If we look at the Bible as somewhat historical, all these books written at different times in different places were really a potpourri of stories and legends and traditions and all finally ended up together in a volume of controversy and many inconsistencies. Almost all the books in the Bible are written with a different style signifying different authors, and since no one knows who wrote these books, there is a lot of conjecture about them and whether or not they were highly edited.

The first five scrolls of the Judaic Bible known as the To-
rah, which are also the first five books of the Old Testament,
seem to be the most intact and unedited. They were reputedly written by Moses, or at least dictated to some scribe
writing down his words. I have personally studied almost every version of the Bible, including Douay-Rheims, King
James, Jerusalem, Lamsa, etc., and even they differ in the
deletion of books and even interpretation. To add the Book
of Revelation was perhaps an action designed by the early
Christians to have their own apocalyptic literature rather
than to rely on the Judaic literature that was apocalyptic in
nature. I guess it's the same principle as Paul being the only
one who came up with the premise that Christ died on the
cross for our sins. Although, as I have stated, Paul never met
Jesus or heard him speak, the early Church forever after took
Paul's idea as gospel. I find it amazing, since Jesus never said
he was going to die for our sins.

Catholic canon law also stated that no one could get
into heaven until Christ's death on the cross. Which means
that they think God kept all the good souls and even
saintly people in some kind of limbo until Jesus died on the
cross, or better yet, none got into heaven even after his

death because none of them were Christians when they died. How mankind can come up with these "laws" is far beyond what I believe is even logical and makes God again humanized; and to even take it further, makes Jesus greater than our Creator.

The Apocrypha was part of the early Church's teachings and "Bible" at one time, as were other religious writings. Then, suddenly, these writers, whose works were originally accepted as infused by God and taught to the masses, are now deemed heretics. Can you imagine yourself back at that time in the midst of a conclave of early Christian leaders and bishops who were bickering over what books would be included in the Bible and being presided over and ruled by a pagan Roman emperor!

You could almost laugh at the ridiculousness of it all, except for the fact that it is so tragic. Tragic in the sense that humankind was deprived of the true outlook on their God . . . tragic in the sense that they were deprived of the true Jesus Christ and his teachings . . . tragic in the sense that a pagan Roman emperor had the last say in the early Church's agenda of conversion by fear for conversion's sake . . . tragic in the sense that so many writings were edited or deemed heretical to satisfy the Church's quest for wealth and power . . . tragic in the sense that humankind, by the influence of the Church, has been made to suffer a dogma of untruth and fear . . . tragic in the sense that the actions of the Church have protected secrets that have perpetuated one of the greatest hoaxes on human-kind . . . and most of all, tragic in the sense that religious teachings today put forth a God to be feared who is judg-mental and puts people in an everlasting hell—not our real God, who is all-loving, all-merciful, all-forgiving, all-powerful, omnipotent and a God who would not let any of His/Her creations be destroyed or suffer everlasting torment in the religiously inspired fantasy of hell.

Humankind have created a conception of God based on their own imperfections. God is the ultimate goodness and it is completely illogical to think that God is perfect and all-loving and then to turn around and give God im-perfect qualities, such as anger or wrath, which send people to an everlasting hell. All of us must question the goodness of ourselves rather than condemning others. It really is a battle within ourselves against the temptations of negativ-ity that we face almost daily in our lives.

CHAPTER 9

The Mystical Traveler

A S I WROTE this book I did not have any fear; but I
also realized that in telling the truth about Our
Lord Jesus Christ, I would be in direct conflict with so
much Christian doctrine as it is put forth today, and of
course the hierarchies and followers of that doctrine. Yet if
you read deeper with your heart open, it is a true belief not
only from years and years of theological research, but from
a common or logical knowledge of who and what our dear
Lord was and also what he did and accomplished.

Jesus Christ was a Jew, and as such his audiences were
mainly comprised of people who were of the Judaic faith.

When he put forth his teachings they were naturally steeped with Judaic overtones and Judaic laws of the time, but his teachings were so universal in nature that they bridged all peoples and all faiths. For example in Matthew 22:36–40 we read, *"Master, which is the great commandment in the Law?" Jesus said to him, "Thou shalt love the Lord thy God with thy whole heart, and with thy whole soul, and with thy whole mind. This is the greatest and the first commandment. And the second is like it, 'Thou shalt love thy neighbor as thyself.' On these two commandments depend the whole Law and the Prophets."* We see that here he is responding to a question from a doctor of Judaic law, and Christ's answer is completely within the framework of Judaic law and yet . . . it is also a universal answer that can incorporate any man and any religion on the face of the earth.

If we took this teaching of Christ at face value and accepted it wholeheartedly, we would eliminate all bigotry and hatred and judgment and condemnation of our fellow man. There would be no persecution of different ethnic and racial groups, or groups that practiced a different religion or groups that were homosexual. It is an act of the greatest hypocrisy to preach these teachings on the one hand and then to turn around and condemn and persecute a racial, ethnic, religious or homosexual group on the other. I personally have seen this done by a supposedly famous religious leader of a conservative Protestant church on television when he bashed homosexuals . . . a leader who professes to believe in and preach the words of Jesus Christ. He evidently doesn't follow the second great commandment that Jesus puts forth in the just-related passage from Matthew. This type of person is what we could call a hypocrite in the truest sense. Hypocrites in general do not practice what they preach and are usually very judgmental and condemning and sometimes persecuting in their nature.

Jesus also had a lot to say about hypocrisy throughout the four gospels. If you substitute the phrase "any religious leader" for the words Scribes and Pharisees, you can see how the following verses in Matthew 23:1–17 are a universal teaching meant for all religions: *Then Jesus spoke to the crowds and to his disciples, saying, "The Scribes and the Pharisees have sat on the chair of Moses. All things, therefore, that they command you, observe and do. But do not act according to their works; for they talk but do nothing. And they bind together heavy and oppressive burdens, and lay them on men's shoulders; but not with one finger of their own do they choose to move them. In fact, all their works they do in order to be seen by men; for they widen their phylacteries and enlarge their tassels, and love the first places at suppers and the front seats in the synagogues, and greetings in the market place, and to be called by men 'Rabbi.' But do not you be called 'Rabbi'; for one is your Master, and you are brothers. And call no one on earth your father; for one is your Father, who is in heaven. Neither be called masters; for one only is your Master, the Christ. He who is greatest among you shall be your servant. And whoever humbles himself shall be exalted. But woe to you, Scribes and Pharisees, hypocrites! because you shut the kingdom of heaven against men. For you yourselves do not go in, nor do you allow those going in to enter. Woe to you, Scribes and Pharisees, hypocrites! because you devour the houses of widows, praying long prayers. For this you shall receive a greater judgment. Woe to you, Scribes and Pharisees, hypocrites! because you traverse sea and land to make one convert; and when he has become one, you make him twofold more a son of hell than yourselves. Woe to you, blind guides, who say, 'Whoever swears by the temple, it is nothing; but whoever swears by the gold of the temple, he is bound.' You blind fools! for which is greater, the gold, or the temple which sanctifies the gold?"*

Christ didn't stop there, he goes on in Matthew 23:23–28 to say: *"Woe to you, Scribes and Pharisees, hypocrites! because you pay tithes on mint and anise and cumin, and have left undone the weightier matters of the Law, right judgment and mercy and faith. These things you ought to have done, while not leaving the others undone. Blind guides, who strain out the gnat but swallow the camel! Woe to you, Scribes and Pharisees, hypocrites! because you clean the outside of the cup and the dish, but within they are full of robbery and uncleanness. Thou blind Pharisee! clean first the inside of the cup and of the dish, that the outside too may be clean. Woe to you, Scribes and Pharisees, hypocrites! because you are like whited sepulchers, which outwardly appear to men beautiful, but within are full of dead men's bones and of all uncleanness. So you also outwardly appear just to men, but within you are full of hypocrisy and iniquity."*

Hypocrisy was a favorite target of Jesus because of its untruth and deception. We find hypocrisy of one form or another throughout our lives, but in the area of religion it does run rampant. When religion puts forth an all-loving and merciful God and then turns around and says to fear God because of His/Her wrath, this is hypocrisy . . . for they say that God is all-loving, merciful and perfect and put that out as truth; then they turn around and betray that truth by saying God is wrathful, vengeful and condemns some of his creations to an everlasting fiery pit to suffer eternally. Just using basic logic, you can't have an all-loving and all-merciful God who then turns around and shows no mercy or love in punishing forever those He/She supposedly loves and shows mercy to.

We also run into religious hypocrisy in the condemnation and judging of supposed "sinners." All religions have differing outlooks on what they consider "sin" and all give various "sins" different classifications of severity. We even have some Christian churches put forth as sin the following: wearing makeup, wearing jewelry, dancing, watching TV, attending movies, women in two-piece bathing suits, mixed swimming, playing cards, smoking, listening to rock music, men wearing beards, unmarried couples kissing, drinking wine in moderation, using a Bible other than King James version, and drinking coffee or tea. When an average adult reads this list, many might laugh at how ridiculous it seems to be, but to certain churches people who do these things are "sinners."

Sin, as I mentioned earlier, is also judged by its severity. In certain religions, adultery by a female (it doesn't seem to apply to the male in most cases) can mean a death sentence. In the case of females in general, sexual sins seem to hold the most stigma, while males get off much more lightly. Many conservative churches still feel that the female is a potential Jezebel who can seduce men with her feminine wiles (hence no makeup, no lipstick, no jewelry, no two-piece swimsuits, etc.). In some cases of sin the female has an advantage, such as in murder, for women are much less likely to get a death sentence than men. Sins in religions are much more likely to daily address the sins of morality rather than crime, especially when it pertains to sexual morality. I guess religions feel that if they can control the sexual morality issues, they can then work on other issues of morality.

I had a woman who used to come regularly to see me as a client. She was a very sweet and caring person, honest, loving and from all outward appearances a very pretty and classy lady. She was also a high-class prostitute. When I told her psychically what she did for a living, she just nodded affirmatively and then told me that she enjoyed her profession, would quit one day when she had her nest egg, marry and hopefully have two children. She was completely nonchalant and very comfortable, and I immediately knew why—she was a good person. Many religions would have strung her up from the nearest tree, so to speak, but she wasn't hurting anybody and did volunteer work at a local hospital. I have always hated the word sin because it is a truly subjective term. Morality is geographical, as women in primitive cultures go around barebreasted and might have several husbands or vice versa. To them it is a traditional way of life and again it harms no one. I have always put forth that what separates a sinner from a nonsinner is motive. If you have the intent to hurt someone, or mean to do harm to someone, you can be judged by your fellow man for criminal intent to maintain social order. But as far as judgment in a religious sense is concerned, no one can judge another soul . . . that is between that soul and God. I personally don't believe in the concept of religious judgment because I know we have an all-loving God who would not hurt or punish anyone. I believe that the only judgment we go through is when we judge ourselves on the Other Side.

With many of the major religions in the world concentrating on humankind's propensity to "sin," they put more emphasis on evil than good. Instead of touting the good deeds that humankind should and could do, they constantly remind their flocks of the bad and evil deeds and inflict guilt to boot. In their negative propaganda, backed up by purported Holy Books that are inconsistent, contradictory and that also emphasize the evils that humankind does, we here on earth are inundated with negative programming. We not only have to watch all the negative news on television programs or read about negativity in newspapers, but we get no solace or respite from our religions. It's no wonder that most of us are stressed, guilt-ridden and exhausted from life. Religion gives us no shelter from the challenges of life and in fact just contributes more by constantly pointing out our sins and giving us guilt.

When my publisher asked me to write this book, I told him that it would be very controversial because with the knowledge and truth that I have garnered over the years, my true representation of Christ would be radically different from that of religion. I hope, if nothing else, whether you agree or disagree, it will set you on a journey to seek your own spirituality and your true sense of knowing who this God-man truly was. Is it true we are all the sons and daughters of God? Absolutely . . . but with this being said, Jesus was a true and divine report or messenger from God. He would be what we refer to as the first and foremost mystical traveler.

What exactly are mystical travelers? They are entities created by God with the perfection to bring about the word of our true all-loving Creator. They are usually assigned to a specific planet to help the creations on that planet evolve their souls. We also can ask to be mystical travelers, but will not attain (at least not in this life) the stature and divineness of Jesus until our souls reach a state of perfection that warrants that designation. Most mystical travelers, as in the case of Jesus, are created with that perfection already intact within them. All mystical travelers, whether they were created as such or attain that state through the evolution of their souls, take a simple oath that they will live their lives in complete service to God and go anywhere to do any good that God infuses them to do.

My Gnostic Christian Church, Novus Spiritus (New Spirit), was founded because we believe that truly all religions have their own messengers or messiahs and ours happens to be Jesus Christ. In many ways Jesus, above all the others, was the most simplistic in his messages and teachings; but he has also been the most misunderstood, argued over and misrepresented messenger or messiah on earth.

Tragically, how is it possible that the teachings of this God-man have gone so badly awry? He taught parables, love, beatitudes, forgiveness, justice and nonjudgment and put forth at that time the new concept of an all-loving, all-merciful and benevolent God. According to the Bible, in his public life he only traveled in a radius of about a hundred miles, and yet his teachings and influence spread eventually throughout most of the world. What or who was it that took teachings of love, formed them into a religion and then turned around and went out and killed millions with their wars, crusades, inquisitions and persecutions?

You probably already know the answer, the early Catholic Church. There has been more horror wrought on humankind in the name of Christianity than of almost all the other religions put together. When early Christianity became the state religion of the Roman Empire in the fourth century, it started to grow by leaps and bounds. With that growth came unbelievable power and corruption.

This kind and caring special messenger named Jesus came into a world maybe not as bad as ours, but very much like ours. A world divided by taxes, the poor, the needy, the rich and the powerful. A world of two warring factions—the Roman Empire and the Sanhedrin, the governing body of Judaic Law and religion.

I'm convinced that Jesus had direct contact with God, with no intermediaries. My guide, Francine, says he had angels in abundance around him and the teachings that he absorbed from tutors in Judaic law as a young boy and from his travels to the Far East also helped him a great deal. But his real guidance came from God.

Certainly as an Essene and Gnostic, Jesus came to show all of us that we have to go through the trials and travails of life that include suffering to learn from life and to magnify our souls. He didn't come to die for our sins (only Paul and the Book of Revelation, which was influenced by Paul, say that), he came to teach and heal and lead an exemplary life doing God's will. His Chart did not allow him, in all his power, to help himself, because he was not a hypocrite, and it also showed that he felt his teachings were the most important part of his life, not his Divinity or power. Although his divinity was magnified in his teachings and power, being incarnated in human form brought out all the frailties and emotions that all of us experience when we incarnate on this plane called Earth. He, like us, fell prey to depression, anger, fear and all the other emotions that we all go through in life in pressing against our written Chart to change it. This manifests in his anger at the moneychangers in the Temple, his fear in the Garden of Gethsemane and his anxiety of feeling alone on the cross when he asked God if He had forsaken him.

One of the controversies that has always surrounded Christ is whether or not he was in actuality Divine. Some believe he was a myth put forth by Christians and Jews and they cite the fact that there are no historical references to Jesus other than in Christian writings. They say that none of the major historians of the time mention anything about the existence of a man known as Jesus Christ, and in actuality this is true. You would think that great historians of the time like Josephus would have mentioned him in their writings, but the truth is that they did not, and it is still a puzzle to many scholars and historians today. Francine says that one reason for this is that Christ's public life was confined to such a small area, and although he drew large crowds of Jews, many did not accept him as a Messiah or the Christ because they were solidly indoctrinated into the Judaic faith that was highly influenced by the Sanhedrin. If indeed Christ had been wholeheartedly accepted by the Judaic people, there would be no Judaic religion today. The Judaic religion had a long history even in Christ's time, and the strength of Judaic tradition and faith overrode the new teachings of Jesus among the vast majority of the people. Yes, Christ had his converts and followers, but most of them still remained loyal to the Judaic faith and became Jewish Christians. You must also remember that during Christ's public life, no semblance or structure of a church or religion had yet formed. The gospels also highly exaggerated his influence on the majority of the followers of the Judaic faith, and were instead used to convert followers of other religions; which is why Jesus sent his disciples to other lands to preach his words.

Many of the Jewish Christians and eventual Gnostics also didn't necessarily believe in his divinity because they knew he survived his crucifixion, did not die and was not resurrected. Most believed he was a great prophet and teacher who carried a message from God and who was human like the rest of them. One of the primary figures of the early Jewish Christian church in Jerusalem was Christ's brother James, who certainly didn't believe in his divinity but certainly did believe that Jesus was a great prophet and messenger with divine teachings for all. Paul and some of Christ's disciples were the ones who really emphasized the divinity of Christ. They initially, by word of mouth, put forth stories of his miracles and teachings in sermons to anyone who would listen. It was not until several decades later that they started to put these stories in writing, and they were definitely slanted from the actual truth to help propagate their new religion that would be called Christianity. As with all religions, they tended to overexaggerate the deeds of their heroes or founders to make a favorable impression that their religion was greater than any other.

In the book *The Templar Revelation—Secret Guardians of the True Identity of Christ,* by Lynn Picknett and Clive Prince, the authors point out an example of how the Gnostics felt about Christ. They write about a doctor whose name was Bernard Raymond Fabré-Palaprat, who allegedly got his authority from what is known as the "Larmenius Charter." Johannes Marcus Larmenius claimed to have written this charter in 1324. He was appointed to be the grand master of the Knights Templar by the supposed last grand master, Jacques de Molay, before he was burned at the stake in 1314 by the Catholic Church and the king of France, who were trying to destroy the Knights Templar. This charter supposedly outlines the continuation of the Order of Knights Templar by containing the signatures of all the subsequent grand masters of the Knights Templar, of which Fabré-Palaprat was now grand master. Fabré-Palaprat also possessed another document of significance called the *Levitikon,* which was a version of John's gospel that had blatant Gnostic overtones and had supposedly been written in the eleventh century. He used the *Levitikon* as the basis for founding the Johannite Church (original Christians) in Paris in 1828, and it certainly had Neo-Templar philosophies.

The *Levitikon* has two parts in its makeup. The first part has religious doctrines that are taught, which include the nine grades of the Templar Order. The second part has much more controversy, as it contains the Gospel of John as it is mainly put forth in the New Testament but omits several significant portions and adds some very contentious writings to it. All of the miracles of Jesus are eliminated, as are certain references to Peter, including the story where Jesus says, "Upon this rock I will build my church." The last two chapters of the original Gospel of John are also eliminated, which refer to his resurrection. In addition, any writing that puts forth that Christ was an initiate of the mysteries of Osiris, the major Egyptian god of his day, and that he had passed on these mysteries and esoteric teachings and knowledge to his disciple John "the Beloved" were included. It also says that Paul and some other Apostles founded the Christian Church, but they did so without any knowledge of Christ's "true" teaching. According to

Fabré-Palaprat, these *secret* teachings that were given to John the Beloved had great influence on the beliefs of the Knights Templar. It also fits in with what my guide Francine says about Jesus learning the "ancient mysteries" in Egypt just before he went into his public life.

What has always been amazing to me is the fact that we have the writings of Christianity on the one hand and, on the other, the equally massive collection of writings from Gnostics and Jewish Christians that, in so many cases, are directly in contradiction. In researching all of these religious writings we can become so confused at the interpretations, discrepancies, omissions, contradictions and blatant falsehoods that it leaves us with our head spinning in wondering who is telling the truth. It really boils down to the premise that if "truth" has been put forth by Christianity, why are there so many adherents of Jesus Christ who have writings against the "truths" of Christianity? If the opponents of Christianity's "truth" were other religions, you could understand their opposition, but other religions don't attack Christianity near as much as the so-called "heretical" sects made up of fellow believers in Christ. A multitude of Christian secret societies throughout history have sprung up, claiming that they have secret knowledge of the real truth about Jesus Christ and Mary Magdalene and Christ's life. Some of these societies became so popular or powerful that the Catholic Church literally tried to suppress them through annihilation in which thousands died.

Why did so many fellow Christians rebel against the teachings and dogma of the early Catholic Church? Could it be that they were based on lies about his death and resurrection and the omission of his true relationship with Mary Magdalene? If truth is put out, you might have a few detractors; but truth is truth and you wouldn't have thousands of fellow Christians fighting those "truths" if they were all really true. There is definitely something fishy going on or, as others like to say, there is something rotten in Denmark.

I have tried to give you the truth as I know it to be. Again, whether you believe what I say or not, we all have to go back not just to the core of faith, because that can be shaken with historical fact . . . but to our real core knowledge that Christ was here on this world and walked among us. Jesus' message was simple. It became complicated because of religion and humankind's need to modify his teachings, change them and omit them for their own agendas of a political and moneymaking nature. Scholars don't know who wrote the four canonical gospels, but it is certainly safe to say that the early Church edited them highly and that they eliminated many other gospels and books that are now contained in what we know as the Apocrypha. These omitted texts held great truths that were kept out of the public eye for centuries. Many of Christ's teachings were edited, such as those on reincarnation and the true nature of God. Many of the facts of Christ's life were omitted or completely made up and exaggerated. Christianity today can condemn an author such as Dan Brown for writing a book of fiction, but they won't condemn themselves for also writing, in many cases, a fictitious account of Jesus Christ.

So with all of this and still carrying Christ as the Messiah in our hearts and soul, what do we do? It's easy—we go on loving and realizing why he came—and, as I stated, he really survived what humankind tried to do to him. His divinity is real and his resurrection was real—it just happened at his real death, when he was eighty-six or so; just as all of us are resurrected at our deaths. Jesus didn't have to die for our sins, nor did he come to die for our sins . . . he came to teach us and give us the knowledge of our all-loving Creator.

Do we celebrate Christmas? Literally for God's sake, I hope so; but maybe, just maybe, it will be a Christmas filled with true joy and the real meaning of Christmas. It doesn't matter what month or date we celebrate it or what anyone says about where he was born or even how he was born. The fact is he came into the world, this world of darkness, then and now and all through the difficult times in which humankind has suffered, fought, survived and died in the last two thousand years . . . and brought a light of hope of the hereafter; and that the true temple of God resides in our soul and our DNA that come from a loving Creator. Easter should also be celebrated with the renewed revival of not only our belief in our Lord but a confirmation of this God-man, who taught love and purpose in our life, and that we are just here to learn and then ascend back home to the Other Side from whence we came.

My Guide told me something so many years ago that I have shared only with my research groups. We know that on the Other Side everyone is happy. But she remembered once that she was listening to a lecture by our Lord, who talks to all of us over there. Francine says during the course of the lecture, he remarked without pain or remorse, but more as a matter of fact, that he had been aware of what would happen after his death; but he had hoped, or at least the human part of him hoped, that humankind would not take his simplistic teachings and turn them into political control and prejudice. He said that, sadly, all everyone seems to remember is a bleeding and bloody figure hanging on a cross . . . not the good works or the healings or the miracles or the love and forgiveness of an all-loving God. Francine says he added, if there is such a thing that people call rapture, it will be the coming of the knowledge of why he came and why he did suffer.

So I wear a cross in honor of Jesus—not one that has him on it in a state of crucifixion; but one that reminds me of the Jesus who lives on in joy and happiness and always walks with us. I am not special, I am only the reporter, not the editor. Only God is the editor. I have to write again that more than any other book I've written, I felt His hand on mine, and when I faltered, it was as if He said, don't stop now, keep on going. So I did.

This Christmas I'm going to gather my family around me and tell them the true story of this God-man, this great and glorious Mystical Traveler who came to bring light to this dark world. I'm also going to encourage them, and all of us, to not just go out and get into a commercial glut, but maybe exchange one gift that we made or something really special and then go out and give of our time to those who don't have as much. Maybe then Jesus wouldn't have lived and eventually died in vain and his words will take root and bloom instead of falling on the barren rocks of our ignorance.

A Note from Sylvia

With so many perspectives on the Bible, I find it important to honor more than one interpretation. *The Mystical Life of Jesus* cites the Bible using translations from the King James and Douay-Rheims versions.

Sylvia Browne is the #1 *New York Times* best-selling author of *Insight; Phenomenon; Prophecy; Visits From the Afterlife; The Other Side and Back; Life on the Other Side; Sylvia Browne's Book of Dreams; Past Lives, Future Healing;* and *Adventures of a Psychic.* She has been working as a psychic for over fifty years, and appears regularly on *The Montel Williams Show.* She has also appeared on *Larry King Live, Good Morning America,* CNN, and *Entertainment Tonight.* She lives in California. Visit her web site at *www.sylvia.org.*